The Decision	
Equipment	8
The Public Carriage Office	11
Manor house station to Gibson Square	16
Map Test	27
Can you call it	31
Back to school	33
Syme versus Sadleir	38
Syme versus Thomas	62
Syme Versus?	70
Twenty-one miles	75
Syme versus Price	84
Déjà vu	92
Sir, Mr, Courtney?	97
A day of being nosey	103
Syme versus Jenkins	109
Oh no O'Connor	116
Still three to go	122
Wobble wobble	127

Now you're with the big boys	132
Oh no, not again	136
To call her Nicola	137
Using my loaf	142
Not what you think	145
Stranger things have happened	151
Monopoly, A geographical nightmare	156
I'm looking at the man in the mirror	161
And then there was light	162
The return of the spatial cowboy	165
Nice n easy my man, nice n easy	167
Just a smile	169
Mr Wilkins, the rematch	171
Mrs Sadleir	173
Mr Jenkins, no truer word spoken	176
Syme versus Thomas	177
Syme versus price, nice price	180
Dutch R.I. P	182
Syme versus Field	184
Not Mrs but Mr Sadlier	186
Syme versus Courtney	188
Syme versus Dixon	192

Syme versus Jenkins	195
Fast Eddie	198
Syme versus O'Connor	200
Let's pretend	201
Syme versus Field	203
Slowly slowly catchy monkey	206
Very very very very nice Price	207
Beyond civilisation	211

The Decision

A Journey of a thousand miles starts with one small step

When I decided to do my knowledge of London, I knew it wasn't going to be easy. I knew that it was going to take discipline, a focused mind and most of all, a lot of hard work. I knew that the Public Carriage Office didn't just give away green badges, the coveted piece of metal that all Licensed London Taxi drivers must possess. I knew that it would be a struggle. I knew that this was a challenge that will one day prove tougher than I thought. What I didn't know, was that my green badge was over six years and forty thousand miles away. In that time, how could I predict punctures, crashes, engine seizures, OK, just the one of those!! numerous 'chats' with the police and winters that Polar Bears would be reaching for scarves. I also didn't realise that through all the hard work and continual disappointment it would eventually be the making of me.

Although there are many contributory factors that made my decision to 'get on my bike' the one thing that has stayed with me throughout my Knowledge is my love of London. I'd always regretted not doing so well at school and longed to further myself academically. I'd seen advertisements for the Open

University and tried to couple my love of London with a suitable degree course that I could knuckle down to. The nearest thing I could find was courses on the history of London. Don't get me wrong, one of the biggest attractions to London is its history but as soon as you sit in a class entitled the History of London you can't move for corduroy jackets and fellas with beards who love a cup of coffee. The last thing I was looking for was sitting in front of a forty-five-year-old bloke banging on about Henry the VIII and how he'd had another disagreement with the missus. I was looking for the sort of knowledge and interest that got the man in the pub talking. Stuff like the statue of Admiral Nelson in Trafalgar square looks down the Mall at his fleet of ships as on top of every lamp post towards Buckingham Palace is a small metal ship of Nelsons victorious army. What about Marble Arch, at the top of Oxford St. used to be the entrance to Buckingham Palace but was later rejected as it was too narrow to get the horses and carriages through on big procession days. It's little stories and anecdotes like that, that have really fuelled my interest and have been a real friend in times of absolute desperation.

I've worked on a fruit and veg stall, in betting shops, various offices and one or two investment banks and all of them jobs had one thing in common, they were all for someone else. I'd always said to myself that if I'd worked as hard for myself as I have for some of those employers, I'd be a millionaire, Well, not so much a millionaire but at least a couple of quid ahead of the bailiffs. Anyway, the need for self-employment and to escape the tyranny of institutionalised life was placed as top priority and a plan needed to be hatched. I would keep my new 'study' a secret from the Investment Bank I was working for at the time. Loose lips sink ships they say.

I had a cunning plan. I would play along with the corporate ladder. Promising to superiors that Banking was for me, that I'd always dreamed of white shirts and various striped pattern cloths. I would aim to be a well-paid student. While keeping the charade going, I'd have to keep a close eye on how much of my time would be needed in various roles at the bank. I don't want to be getting too good at anything if you know what I mean. I'd known for a while that managerial roles weren't all they were cracked up to be.

Most of the time, the supervisory roles were quite labour intensive and leaving the office late at night is a common occurrence and filled only by those that have their sights set firmly on the proverbial dangling carrot. Most of the time that carrot is being dangled by a non-too reassuring past holder of the role looking for more time away from the daily drudge themselves. 'Step up to the plate' 'There is no I in TEAM' 'if you want to change the world you have to start with the man in the mirror'. You know the drill.

So, I weighed it all up, took down my dart board of everything that concerned me about drifting towards retirement in a white partitioned office and went to bed, I'd done a lot of thinking. I woke up the day after my great revelation and thought what now? Well, I needed freedom. I needed something that would complement my love of conversation. A challenge that would involve my love of London and that, over the course of time, would hopefully teach me a little more than how to order stationery.

My mum's uncle was a black cab driver and all I ever saw him do was drink tea in my nan's kitchen. I'd heard a few stories of when the financial exchange LIFFE folded up its trading floors in favour of computerised dealing that a lot of the redundant traders went on to do the knowledge. This was shrouded with the slightly unfair rumours that LIFFE traders weren't skilled in anything apart from shouting and waving their arms about and therefore cab driving was an ideal vocation. Scandalous I know. Well, some of them did get on their bikes and did get the knowledge done and are out there now, once again, throwing their arms about but this time it's about the Aldgate one way system rather than the Tokyo Stock Exchange. I suppose this attitude was also an attraction to my decision. I wanted to prove to myself that I was going to become one of those self-managers. Someone you could leave in a room with the bits to an Air fix model and come back to find a World War two Spitfire sitting on your coffee table, even if the picture on the box was of a Mississippi paddle steamer.

So, there it was. I'd found my challenge. My London degree was going to be The Knowledge. This was going to be easy, very easy. Learn a few roads. Find out where South London is and pick up my green badge at the Public Carriage Office Licences window and spend the rest of my life with my right arm slightly browner than my left. Alright, my calculations were slightly wrong.

The Equipment

Fail to prepare and you prepare to fail.

As they said in Monty Pythons film Life of Brian, 'what did the Romans ever do for us?' Well, again from that film the answer was, apart from sanitation, they gave us roads. Picture the scene two thousand years ago. A few Romans relaxing in their local baths discussing last night's feast and yesterdays' gladiatorial battle when one turns around and says, "It was a nightmare getting here today you know". The second Roman grabs his robe from a stone hook and replies, "well it's because of all the stones and rocks knocking about in the fields". A third Roman interjects, "You know what we need, some kind of smooth, dedicated Chariot path to get us from the dwellings to the Coliseum because if I lose another wooden wheel". It was from a conversation like this that the Romans gave us a whole network of roads, but it was over the next two thousand years that the labyrinth that is now London developed. Until you see them, how can you explain to the novice that there are some roads in London that you can't get a car through. There are alleyways in the City that you can just about get people through. There are over a thousand no stopping zones. Hundreds of Blue Plaques on buildings telling the reader who lived there at which period and what they are famous for. Understanding all the mind-boggling one-way systems and no entry signs would drive you to the point of madness if you attempted to do the knowledge in a car. The first and most vital piece of study equipment you need is the trusty moped.

Motorbikes are OK I suppose, but considering the number of miles you cover and the unpredictability of the journey ahead facing all those seasons and prejudging all those Sunday drivers, you can't go wrong with a moped. The most trustworthy and most recognisable knowledge bike that ever made its way from North to South London has got to be the Honda C90. To those of you who don't lie awake at night drooling over waterproof jackets, wishing one day of achieving fifty miles an hour on the speedometer, it's a pizza delivery bike without the deep pan box. Why the Honda C90? It's extremely economical, why do you think it's the chosen road burner of Malaysia and Thailand. If ever you get a puncture, they're one known fault, there isn't a mechanic in the land who doesn't know how to fix them. Which is quite handy considering the first time I ever made it to Streatham Common from my home in Epping, I got a puncture on the high road and had to wheel it into a back street bike mechanics that only dealt with very big bikes. I remember wheeling my little bike into the calendar papered workshop with a tear in my eye looking for a greasy, tattoo ridden hells angel to take pity on me and get me back on the road within minutes. Such a quick turnaround is not uncommon to expect with a C90 seeing as they are lesson one on the bike mechanics training course.

There is also the, dare I say it, street credibility of others knowing that, with a board stuck on the handlebars, you're a knowledge boy, which usually means you're living a life of uncertainty and continual bewilderment.

This can help in various ways. Drivers letting you weave through the traffic. People turning a blind when you suddenly need to stop as you've just missed where Brahm Stoker lived and wrote Dracula. The Knowledge bike with a mounted board with the routes (runs) on is also a great conversation starter. As every knowledge boy will tell you, there is a slight gulf between the badge holding, qualified cab driver and the struggling, know nothing knowledge boy. It's like the student never questioning the master. although there is a good deal more drivers that still hold out a flame for their days of trying to find a small park in the pouring rain while warming frozen hands-on exhaust pipes. This transforms itself in the form of conversations while sitting at traffic lights. It's a very encouraging thing when a man of seventy spurs you on by telling you to "keep going son, it's a good living, I've loved it". Like when I pulled up alongside a cab at the lights in Gray Inn Road in Clerkenwell, soaking wet from top to toe, with rain running down my backside and the cab driver giving away the little gem of "Well, when your wet your wet". Although he'll never write a thesis on philosophy, I don't think you can argue with that.

The Public Carriage office –
The final bastion of the British empire.

OK, so what's all this about purgatory, hardship, and continual struggle, well, let me explain. The knowledge is the study of every road, street, alley way and one way system within a six-mile radius of Charing Cross, The Helena Cross to be precise, in the quest to become a London Black Taxi Driver. It's a radius of six miles as the 'Lord high protector' Oliver Cromwell back in 1652, English Civil war, said that our military defence were built this far around the capital. Mr Cromwell thought that it would be far too dangerous for Hackney Carriages to venture beyond this point. Some of the old boys still think that now when they're asked to go to Peckham. OK, he took away Christmas, but he looked after the cab drivers. The Public Carriage Office, who govern over knowledge candidates, also require you to know all foreign embassies, public buildings, historical places of interest, public houses, hospitals, police, fire and ambulance stations. In fact, to put it bluntly if it's in London, you need to know it. It's not uncommon at certain stages of your examinations that you will be asked to name all the roads ran in the London marathon, in the order of being run or to name every country that vote in the EU referendums and where their embassies are based in London. Admittedly, these questions are some of the more bizarre I've seen on the knowledge although when someone jumps in the back of a cab and say's "Driver, I need to visit the nearest horse saddlery shop and before we get there, I need a cash machine" your knowledge will be tested.

Anyway, back to the purgatory and hardship of the poor old knowledge student. Once you are initially accepted on the knowledge of London, after a doctor's medical form and application given to the public carriage office in Islington, you are invited for your initial talk.

The talk is a general overview of what is required from you and how you will be tested. It is at this initial talk at the carriage office where the forty or so candidates gathered in the room are reliably informed that statistics show in three years from that date, there will only be three of you still doing the knowledge. The dropout rate in massive. The amount of people that think "I know, I'll do my knowledge, pass out and go and earn a few quid" are very much surprised at the amount of work needed to drive a London cab hence the dropout rate. Once you are actively living the life of the Knowledge student, you must have the grip of a Russian weightlifter to hold on. This will be mainly due to the lack of syllabus within the study of the knowledge. It's unique in the fact that once you learn your 'Blue Book', which is the standard set of four hundred routes that you are required to know verbatim, the rest is up to you. Once you have covered enough ground you apply for your map test. This written test consists of three lots of three routes. In each set of three, they all go to the same place.

Two of the routes will have errors in. It's up to you to spot the correct route obviously assuming you know the start and the finish as well. The best bit of the map test is the map itself. You are given a blank map of an area where your only clue is two road names written on. It's up to you to find the three or four road names that your examination paper is asking for. See how the games have already started?

You don't only need to know where you're going but here you need to know what those roads look like and the shape of them on a blank map. If you get past this stage of the knowledge the next stage is where the fun starts. Get the tissues ready and eat plenty of fish for that brain because you are entering the appearance stage. An 'Appearance' is how your knowledge will be tested by the Public Carriage Office examiners. You are required to 'Appear' in front of an examiner face to face to recite every road from a destination of their choice to a second destination of their choice. Initially, your appearances will be 56 days apart, the beginning. At each appearance you have the chance to score a D (no points) C (three points) B (four points) or the coveted A (six points). You need to build up a total of 12 points from seven appearances to move onto the next stage where you are required to appear every twenty-eight days. You usually find the further you get to stage three, which is twenty-one-day appearances, the trickier routes and bizarre questions start to flow. Twenty-eight-day appearances are where your knowledge is really being tested. You never know what part of London, or which places you will be tested on in any appearance, but the heat is turned up on "28's". You never know what question or situation the examiner will require you to have knowledge of. You just know that you better start to get to know everything that was, or is, in London because you've only got about 10-15 minutes in an appearance to prove it. The examiner needs to know that you have been out on your bike at least once. Before your first appearance, you've most probably been out on your bike a couple of hundred times and already have a minor aversion to manhole covers. Just imagine studying structural engineering for four years at university. You've covered every weight, measurement and problem-solving situation only to sit in front of your examiner and get asked the maiden name of the mother of the man that built the Severn bridge, "oh, you don't know? well, come back in 56 days and I might just ask you again, then again, I might not!". I wouldn't be surprised to see SAS interrogation experts taking notes in some appearances sooner or later. Again, this type of study system, where you just don't know what's around the corner, conditions the mind to expect the unexpected. To say "thank you Sir/ma'am" when you have just been told you haven't got a chance in passing the knowledge with your current work rate which is already every waking hour. So, three stages of appearances decreasing in time apart, 56, 28 and 21 days to reach the nirvana of 'The suburbs. This is where you are finally required to have, at the very least, a reasonable to good understanding of routes and areas the exist outside the six-mile radius you spent so long studying. These will include a thorough understanding of Heathrow airport and a chance to look at pratts bottom....in surrey. There are one hundred and thirty routes stretching far and wide taking in most suburbs North, East, South and West of central London. You have six weeks to learn all these routes and will be tested on at least ten of them on your very final appearance.

You are required to address your examiner as Sir, Ma'am or Miss, getting these mixed up wouldn't be a wise move and it can be safely assumed you just scored yourself a D before you've even sat down. You'll attend dressed in a suit and tie and clean shaven, just for men that last requirement. I suppose this is where the term 'Appearance' comes into its own. As you must have gathered by now, undertaking the knowledge will inevitably teach you more than roads. It has been said that the Public Carriage is one of the last bastions of the old British empire and when you've experienced the trials and tribulations of this anarchic study you can't help but fill you are required to show that 'stiff upper lip'. In the face of all adversity, you are constantly reminded of the old saying that character isn't judged on how you fall but how you get up again. Well, there you go. Hopefully I've given you some kind of idea how it all works, how you're judged, and the possible pitfalls of the journey undertaken.

So, if you are on the verge of treating a decision to do 'your Knowledge' lightly, think again. Sit down, take a deep breath and fill the forms out carefully, black ink please. If you do decide to take the first steps on this dark, scary road, I'd like to give you the best piece of advice that all students are reliably told by examiners and cab drivers alike during their study. Described best in the picture of the Stork with a frog halfway eaten in its beak. All you can see of the frog are its legs hanging out of the stork's mouth. One more gulp and that's the end of the frog. The only thing preventing this from happening is the frog's hands have managed to stay out of the Storks beak and fix themselves firmly around the Stork's neck. The message at the bottom of the picture is NEVER GIVE UP.

Manor house station to Gibson Square, It begins.

Never judge a (blue) book by its cover

I'd made the decision on Saturday. That night was like going to bed before a big holiday. The feeling of excitement and new beginnings. Not knowing what the imminent future holds. Wondering whether you should just go to sleep in your travelling clothes, just to be ready to go as soon as your eyes open. Sleeping with your passport on your chest and a plane ticket under your chin. I woke up on Sunday morning or rather just stepped out of bed fully clothed and thought I can't wait for Monday I'll have to do something today. The very first run on the standard Blue Book is Manor House tube station in Finsbury Park North London to Gibson Square in Islington. So, with the thought of no time like the present, I got on my five-gear push bike and set off. It was a lovely day, t-shirt weather as they say. Although I knew I wasn't obviously going to continue to do the knowledge on a push bike the biggest thing of that day was that no matter how I done it, I'd started my knowledge.

I'd been advised by my trusty friend and confidant Jeff that John's Scooters in Dalston Lane, Hackney was the only place to get all my equipment in one go. Johns was the kind of motorcycle shop that understood the path of the Knowledge boy. They knew you didn't have time to breathe before needing to get back out on that bike and see more of London. If you walked in there with one of the top ten things that go wrong with Knowledge bikes, i.e., Honda C90's, you'd be seen within twenty minutes and out on the road within forty. Johns wasn't the kind of place you took the family to browse around though. Some of the language on a busy day in there would make a boxing promoter blush. It was the kind of shop come garage where not only were the mechanics covered in oil but, the dog too. One thing old John, the owner, missed out on though was the silver-tongued delivery of the cheap suited after salespeople. This was another attraction of shopping at John's. Much the same as the diners who know the evening won't be one of the politest when faced with the waiters of Soho's famous Chinese restaurant Wonkies. As although the food that gets served there is some of the best in Chinatown, the waiters are known for their curt and abrupt attitude towards diners. This is known and has become part of the Wonkies experience. I've been told to 'Hurry up' 'sit down' and, quite the norm if arriving as a couple or three, placed on a table of other diners just to fill up the spaces, only Wonkies have that licence. The best thing about talking to old John about bikes though was that he'd seen it all before and his replies were evidently loaded with boredom. I remember the extent of his after sales treatment was after putting the money I'd given him, under his old till, as I wheeled 'Dutch' onto Dalston lane to hear him shout 'Don't forget to sling some oil in it every now and again or you'll kill it'. John's Scooters isn't there now in Dalston Lane but as with all those that give character and experience to a situation, he's missed and I only hope that the flame of the no nonsense, oil covered workshop is being held across the land by other Motorbike shops. I must say that I always thought it a strange British thing that we do in naming Cars or much worked machinery but without realising it I'd fallen for this myself. Being that the number plate on my 'brand new' Honda C90 ended with the letters KLM, Jeff thought it only fitting that 'her' name should be taken from those letters of the Dutch Airline and therefore Dutch was christened. I Knew that naming cars was a habit taken on by seventy-year-old Morris Minor owners who'd come through thick and thin with old 'Rosey'. Young wavy-haired girls driving around in old VW beetles were also prone to the naming of vehicles as they'd had 'sooo much fun in Becky'. I knew I'd be going through a few years of muck and bullets doing the knowledge and sometimes it would be beneficial to have something to relate your thoughts to even if that trusty companion comes from Japan and has an engine for a stomach.

As with all beginners, I was loving the bike work. Going out there, seeing parts of London you've only ever seen on the News and picking up more and more information on every trip. The weather always surprising you and the sites constantly changing. Seeing different people being themselves on the streets corners of which they lived. Realising that other areas and communities existed without me ever stepping foot in them has always fascinated me. Just when you think you know your own area and the people in it. Just when you've grown up with all your own areas history and rumour and fun and disaster there's a whole new world around the corner. A world in which you have no idea of the local 'in' jokes or the places that you wouldn't normally go after dark. Areas of beauty that amaze you and force you into stopping the bike for a longer look. How can anybody go to Greenwich for the first time and not stop to see where Admiral Nelson learnt the ropes of sea command. To travel through the old meat market at Smithfield in the City and not wonder of times past. Seeing the William Wallace blue plaque in the corner there and thinking as you cross London Bridge that when he was captured his fate was to be hung, drawn, and quartered with his head being impaled on the spikes of the old bridge for all to see.

I knew that if I read about London at the same time as doing my knowledge, not only would I get to see all these historic places I'd know why as well.

There was the thought also that it might see me through those times sitting in the rain in a place I'd never been before wondering if it was all worth it. Every time I went out on my bike was like the beginning of a small adventure. For someone who's always wanted to travel the world living out of a suitcase, and arrive home windswept and interesting, the knowledge was proving a dam good substitute.

Dr Johnson said that "those who are tired of London are tired of life, for London has all life can afford". I couldn't agree more. From the old West Indians sitting and laughing on their door fronts in Notting Hill to groups of fashion-conscious women drinking spritzers on the Kings Road the cultures are forever changing. Once I'd been out on my bike a few times the change in culture and area was almost tangible. The driving attitude through Brixton's densely populated Atlantic Road is notably more friendly than the frantic gateway to Heathrow at Hammersmith's Broadway. It has always struck me that local driving is always more relaxed. People know where they are going. When you get to main gateways heading somewhere where most people only visit you are faced with other drivers panic and uncertainty. This leads to rash driving decisions and eventually from a couple of toots on the horn, road rage. Some areas, although miles from where you've come from instantly feel like you'd be ok to live there while others just don't have that 'mothers cooking' feel about them. New York is a place that, although very different from London, has that 'I could live there' feel. The weather always separates the tryers from the non tryers and London's weather is no different. I've sat on my bike in all different areas of London and noticed that certain areas feel better with certain weather. This sounds crazy I know but I don't think you can walk through life just being a certain kind of weather person. You've got to fit the bad in with the good. There's no better feeling than to have a wet face at West India pier in the Docklands. To have a chill from the riverside of Narrow Street in Wapping on a stormy day when the world looks like it's going to end is one of those pure 'I'm alive' feelings. Trafalgar Square, with fountains at full blast and all and sundry trying their luck at paddling in Central London on a blisteringly hot day is amazing to see. Seeing the acres of land at Hampstead Heath covered in snow on a winter's morning. Spotting foot and paw prints and thinking I should have been earlier to make this view perfection. Weather, like a lot of adversity, is an attitude. Like the saying 'there's no such thing as bad weather just wrong clothing'. Obviously, I'm talking with rose tinted glasses due to my love of London, but you have to agree, certain weather at a certain time, in the right situation, can make your heart sing. It says in the Bible, seek and ye shall find and I make it right. If you're looking for diverse weather, then get yourself to London.

It's quite easy to ramble on about any subject which you love but there is an art in finding beauty in the most horrid of places and situations. It's a skill that you must train your brain to do. An overall outlook on life. Like seeing people pull themselves up out of the most adverse times with character and strength is always admirable. They say that it's not how you fall but how you get back up again and apart from bung taking boxers, it's something worth remembering. I've always tried to find that hidden beauty in the most unlikely of places on my bike as the number of times you'll be sitting in a traffic jam during a day in London is quite often. It's not so hard to see the good side of life sitting in a traffic jam at Tower Bridge as you're waiting for the bridge master to raise the road so a big ship on the Thames can pass under. It's a little more difficult to see the melancholy side of our existence when that same traffic jam is stuck right in the middle of a backstreet in Shoreditch and all you can see is wheelie bins and pigeons. Then again, I was once sitting in Cable Street waiting for a truck to deliver a package and happen to observe a drunk man explaining to two rats where they were going wrong in life. That put a smile on a few faces. What's more, at one point, it looked like the rats might have had a valid point. East London rats see, very strong opinions.

Again, there in Cable Street, what more history could I have been sitting around waiting for that truck. Cable Street, East London was the area where the fascist leader Sir Oswald Mosley took about three hundred and fifty likeminded fascists through this street in the 1930's to protest at the Jewish population's settlement in East London. There were about a hundred thousand Jewish living in the Whitechapel area at the time and rumour has it that most of them were around Cable Street on that day to counter protest Mosley's march. The police tried hard to keep some kind of order but as the march made its way west towards the City, they say the violence started to take on an almost war like feel. Reports have been written of Dockers and ship workers making their way over from the Docklands to side with the Jewish. They say there were Dockers of all nations armed with pickaxes and all manner of self-made weaponry side by side with normal every day Jewish folk. The thought of the famous 'Battle of Cable Street' as it's now known being right there where the truck was holding up all the traffic gave my mind a more gallant feel for those waiting minutes.

You don't have to do all this reading and history searching doing the knowledge, but I just found it something that was part of me to do. There are some knowledge students out there that find doing the knowledge easy. They are there just to learn the roads, get their direction straight and pick up their green badges. Some of them couldn't tell you who lived in Buckingham Palace but wouldn't see a problem in knowing where a four-foot alley way is eight miles away in Southeast London. After all, the Public Carriage Office aren't looking for London historians, they're looking for cab drivers and the funny thing is, so are the passengers. By the time knowledge students 'pass out' and become Licensed London taxi drivers they have built up such a knowledge of the city it's difficult to see what they don't know. At the height of study on the Knowledge you'll name the location of around 5,000 public places, just as many roads, streets, alleyways, and squares, tell who lives there and who's buried where. All this while pondering the unsolved mystery of wet underwear through waterproof clothing in the rain at Vauxhall Cross.

In New York, as Long as you can speak reasonable English and drive a car you can become a yellow cab driver. I even think the rule of reasonable English gets overlooked the majority of the time thinking of my experiences of New York and their cab drivers. In Australia, if you have a rough knowledge of the immediate area, are courteous and drive safely you are granted a local cab licence. In India, going on the rate of fatalities on the roads out there I think the rule for acceptance is if you sit in the right seat, you're on.

No other city in the world demands such high standards from cab drivers than London and thank heavens they do. The bike work while doing the knowledge is physically tiring. It exposes you to all weathers. It teaches you to work smarter rather than harder although in the beginning of your Knowledge, harder is preferred. You have to pre-plan your journey and your work. What you must see, what you have to learn is always urgent and time is always an issue as your next appearance is constantly looming. Then there's the repetition of calling the roads you have travelled and practicing one-way systems and the never-ending map reading. In the beginning, the map of London is daunting. It is difficult to see in the more densely populated parts and there are always areas that you need to 'run your finger over'. At the height of your work, midway through your knowledge, the map becomes a friend. Something you have seen a thousand times. Something you always refer to in times of uncertainty. The map has all the answers. Consult the map.

To familiarise myself with the map more I would play games like asking anyone who'd listen to call out the name of any road from the London A-Z and, with my eyes closed, would attempt to put my finger on that road on the map. David Blaine eat your heart out. Most of the time I could get this little trick exactly right but when I didn't this would cause a sudden rush of directional panic and lead to about an hour of rehearsing that area and all ways in and out of it.

Those in the wings

No book on the knowledge would ever be complete without mentioning what is known in the game as the Knowledge Widow. The title is self-explanatory but more of a thank you to those thousands of Knowledge widows who assist in the terminal pain in the search for the Green Badge. Whether they be Wives, Girlfriends, Boyfriends, Mums, dads or even, for that matter, anything depending on the physical and mental presence of the knowledge boy/girl, I have to say a heartfelt thank you. Children, pets, employers, social occasions, and the odd romantic date are all subject to the loss of someone dear to them for the length of time it takes to accomplish the Knowledge. Every minute of the day is taken up by being out on your bike, looking at the map or spent in the company of other such lost souls. Every time you fall off your bike. Every time you don't score on an appearance. Every time you think it's not worth carrying on, these modern-day martyrs must pick up the pieces. There they are with the emotional bandages and hot cups of tea constantly offering that proverbial shoulder to cry on. They arrive at times of much needed support and when all is well and healed drift off into the night like caped crusaders. As the knowledge Student awakes from the nightmare of not remembering where the American embassy is or gazing at the flat rear wheel tyre, they are oblivious to the level of support given by the Knowledge widow.

Their only concern is how can you do a right hand turn off Knightsbridge into Hyde Park?

Seriously though, to you all, thank you.

MAP TEST

I failed my first map test. It was Streatham, Southwest London. In I went, full of nerves thinking I can't even get through the West End fluently let alone wondering what area will be under this test paper when I'm told I can 'turn over now'. As soon as I saw the map was on Streatham, I knew that my size nines were going to find this mountain a bit too steep. There's an old, and unfair, saying in the black cab game that cab drivers hardly ever go south of the river Thames. I'm sure that drivers who come from South London don't mind it at all but anyone north of the river seems to lean on the fact that South London is always a bit sticky to digest in the mental region. Streatham? I'm from Kentish Town NW5, what would I ever know about Streatham. Even the residents of the Streatham area would rather be tested on somewhere North of river, I'm sure. As with all exams the world over, when you see the paper, you know if you don't know, and you know if you do. The ironic thing about exams is just at a time when you need to hold your nerve the most you realise your nerves have totally gone, well that or they've been taking Salsa lessons. I didn't reach the required pass mark which I think was about seventy percent, aren't they all?

I had to wait about two months for my next Map test. This is one of the things about the knowledge that a few years down the line really separates the men from the boys (or the girls from the Women), the time between being seen again and getting another go. It's a great test of stamina and a good leveller as well. Even the superstar knowledge students have to wait patiently for their next appearance. I can honestly say that it becomes so evident that all are treated the same up the carriage office. No special cases and all are welcome to endure the purgatory.

As the fifteen of us walked in single file, see? regimental, to the main examination room at the end of the corridor I felt a little better about my knowledge. I knew I'd done a lot more work in preparation for this one and looking around didn't seem as nervous as some of the sorry souls taking their seats. As the examiner chosen to supervise the Map test walked around handing out, face down, the papers I looked around the room. I could see one or two that I recognised from my first test. I remember thinking that a little sun bed or a vitamin course would have been beneficial to some of these worried, pale faces. We sat waiting for the examiner to announce the start. Almost like the lull before the storm, there was a peace in the room. It's usually at situations like this I think of a something that makes me giggle like a naughty schoolboy. The thought of at least one of the more nervous of us being overcome by this silent lull and slowly slipping out of their chair and laying face up, breathing slowly made me hold my stomach through laughter. Luckily for us all, this didn't happen, and the examiner raised his head from the front desk and told us we had 50 minutes to complete all questions and the map picture….and then leave. You wouldn't want some of these examiners as uncles I can tell you.

I turned over and, as I said, you know if you know. Baker Street, lovely. I'd seen mock maps of Baker Street only the day previous to the test and knew I had a good chance of passing. Everything went right. I spotted the errors on the routes and knew most of the places they wanted me to pinpoint. I even wrote every answer to all the questions on the back of the paper just in case my pen had slipped, and I picked the wrong boxes on the multiple-choice questions. I left the exam room feeling like I was moving towards a true understanding of the capital, yeah, I know what you're thinking, but just let me live the dream for a moment. It had been about a week, and I'd heard nothing from the carriage office. We were told we'd be informed of our results within this time. So, I rang them. Sometimes there's no better feeling than to stumble across good fortune. I rang the carriage office and, after getting through the labyrinth of pre-recorded multiple choices, got through to a real person. In fact, it seemed I'd got through to the person responsible for sending out the results, proving those prerecord choices really did get you to the right department. Good old-fashioned efficiency. As I hinted towards advising him that maybe their postal set up was slightly behind, he spoke saying 'who? Mark what? yes, I have it right here'. You just don't get coincidences like this and not get the result you want. Before I could ask if the letter had been sent, he just said 'oh yes, you've passed, I'm just sending it out now'. Passed? this was it, the beginning. I was on the path. My first 56-day appearance would be round in no time, well, alright, 56 days for those paying attention. I'd better start looking at colours of cabs, because silver seems to be the new black of late. What about a badge holder, do I get the leather one that hangs around your neck or the small one that clips onto your shirt pocket because all cab drivers' must 'display the badge at all times'. Ok, I didn't consider I could be five years away from these kinds of decisions but like a roaring hot day in the middle of October, get your shirt off, it won't last for long.

CAN YOU CALL IT?

Put your Knowledge where your mouth is

My first appearance was about two weeks away. Two weeks to get as much work done as possible before the given date. This was probably just enough time to for my celebratory 'map test' hangover to disappear. All the work you put in on your bike, seeing points, roads and areas means nothing if you can't remember it when you're not there. To remember all this information, you must constantly rehearse, like actors with stage lines, when the curtain goes up, you're live. They say that when you first 'go up' you'll surprise yourself and you'll know more than you thought. For instance, they'll ask you the royal society of OB's and GOB's (obstetricians and gynaecologists) to Admiral Nelsons jacket (displayed in the National maritime museum, Greenwich). You'll hear this from the examiner and in pure robotic form crack straight into it, Regents Park to Greenwich, let's go. Well, that's what they say but, yes, you do know more of London when tested but if there is anything to stop nerves, pre-exam time, then it's still under a rock in the Himalayas, because it hasn't been found yet. I don't know the number of subscribers to Weight watchers in this country but my advice to those who seek a smaller waistline is get yourself on the knowledge. Pre-exam nerves materialises in many forms and visits to the toilet on the morning of an appearance can be cause for family concern. You've been on your bike for about 18 months to two years, had the map of London up on the kitchen wall for all that time and can name every left turn onto Oxford Street going south. On the morning of your appearance, you'd struggle with who the fella standing on top of the column in Trafalgar Square is.

Who lives down the Mall in the 'big house' at the end is a complete mystery. It's all well and good doing all the work but the true test comes in that appearance room. There are all different ways you can rehearse your knowledge. I've tried it on my own, ripping up small pieces of paper and drawing them out of a hat so as I don't know what's coming. I've tried writing out runs ten times so as I become fluent with those routes much in the same way that schoolteachers, as punishment, would order you to write out lines so as you understand the meaning of a certain rule. If you're going to 'call' on your own, you must be imaginative. Although, at one point during my study, I resorted to placing a dinner plate on a cushion on my lap and pretending the plate was the steering wheel and I had real people jumping in my cab (which was the sofa) and instructing me to go somewhere. To which, I'd reply, 'ok sir' and turn the 'steering wheel' accordingly. I was almost in full conversation with some of my fictitious passengers. Complaining of the one-way system in the Kitchen and how the congestion charge hasn't affected any of the traffic in the upstairs hallway. Occasionally I'd receive a generous tip as

I dropped them off outside the downstairs toilet. Alright, I must admit, the 'dinner plate' idea was about three years into my study and, as you can tell, insanity was doing its best to become my new friend. I don't generally recommend this technique as a study tool.

Back to School

The one true way to study and test your knowledge pre-appearance time has got to be at one of the Knowledge schools that operate in London. Knowledge schools are the Mecca for students. Full to the brim with likeminded (mad) knowledge boys and girls sitting around desks covered with the map of London eagerly trying to get from A to B in a straight line. The map on the desk is covered with a sheet of Perspex to which the student asking the questions will draw on with a marker pen the roads the other student is calling out. Only after the student calling has finished and got to their destination will both look at the route taken and examine, learn, and even re-arrange that route or 'line' to a better if not perfect standard. This is where you find out what your made of so far. Sometimes, you can sit in front of your call over partner, listen to the question for example "take me from Thierry Road SW17 to the stage door of the dominion theatre", and confidently call out loud every road from point to point. As your partner takes the pen away from the map you both sit back and look at the route taken. It's only then you realise you've just called what looks like the route taken by Phileas Fogg to get around the world in eighty days.

Knowledge Schools are obviously fall of characters. Usually your 'strange' and 'misguided' route you took from the above would usually be greeted with something warm hearted and understanding like a raw of laughter. Meanwhile your partner voices his supportive opinion bleating out 'are you doing this knowledge by the London underground?'. You can't beat a knowledge school for information and the sharing of ideas. It's the same for any school, college, etc but I think Knowledge students are slightly different. I don't think many university students spend all day in the rain, wearing what looks like deep sea fisherman clothing, listening to men in white vans speculate loudly on your sexual orientation and what you like to do in your spare time. Only then, after the physical work has been done, is it off to knowledge school and try to recite every road, main building, and most of the smaller ones within the largest city in Europe. There is certain etiquette that should be taken note of in knowledge schools. Noise is obviously a big factor. The knowledge can be quite a tough time for some, if not, all students. With the school becoming the only place they can build confidence and absorb all the information needed the last thing you want is a load of others talking loudly and disrupting your concentration. Whenever this kind of thing used to happen when I was a kid, the teacher would step in and politely ask the offenders to quieten down and carry-on reading. When this kind of thing happens at a knowledge school it's usually greeted with a forty-year-old man throwing a board marker at someone's head and, very impolitely, telling them unless they value their wedding tackle, they'd better respect the need for peace, amen. I've obviously exaggerated that a bit, but you understand my point, you need to be zoned into this knowledge or you find that you won't score as quickly as some of the other students. As someone once said, 'The harder I work, the luckier I get'. Another hidden etiquette in the schools, usually instructed by the person running the place, is to put people together who are at the same level in their knowledge and appearances. It's no good putting a person on 21-day appearances with someone who has just started the Knowledge.

When you're in your prime your quicker, and you start to assume that some things don't even warrant a mention because they're so obvious to the trained eye. So, as the person on 21's flies through a route because he's done it a thousand times before, the poor old beginner can't even find the first three roads they've called out and thereby slowing down the whole work progress for the advance person. Meanwhile, the beginner doesn't get any discussion of the route or roads as they would have done from someone of a similar level. The early days of your Knowledge school attendance are all about discussing the routes, roads and rumours. You hear a hundred questions a day in a school. 'Can you turn left there?' 'Is this a one way?' 'Do you take one sugar or two?' the list is endless. And with every question, from somewhere in that room, will come the answer and thereby furthering your knowledge.

When you're a little bit more advanced, the questions become less and less. When you're at the end of your 21-day appearances and already taking your cab driving test, the questions are virtually non-existent and all your worried about then is getting through the daily point sheets. Apart from the Blue Book, point sheets are one of the very few structured learning tools on the knowledge. So, other than saying 'Knowledge boy, go learn London' point sheets at least give you an indication of what the Public Carriage Office examiners are asking daily. Basically, a point sheets is all the questions asked that day from examiners up the carriage office. All these daily questions are gathered by other knowledge boys with clip boards who hang around the front entrance of the carriage office waiting for Knowledge boys who have just had an appearance to walk out and spill all. 'What examiner did you get?', what did they ask you? To this you reply with all the questions you were asked in your appearance. All this information is gathered up by the 'points collectors' and whisked off to their associated knowledge school and, hot off the press, are then circulated around the thousands of hopeful knowledge students, for a fee obviously, we've all got to eat!

There then follows a mass panic from all knowledge boys to see if they can complete the sheets of questions, i.e., calling the routes asked and highlighting any points of interest on the sheet that they don't already know. It is from these sheets that you can attempt to keep up with what's being asked and what the examiners are expecting you to know. Anything on these sheets that you don't already know you'll go out on your bike and see it for yourself. Obviously, it starts to be a cat and mouse game between the examiners and knowledge students, as they are asking about places that have or are just being built, so you must stay topical. If the Phantom of the opera moves from Her Majesty's theatre in the Haymarket to the Palace theatre in Cambridge Circus, you better know about it or you may as well be a bottle of five-day old milk, in other words…. you're out of date.

The point sheets are a great source of discussion and an endless guider to further your knowledge. I've seen questions like the more common, 'give me every left turn off Oxford st going from east to west to some more obscure questions like calling a route from Harrods to the New Kings Road without ever seeing a set of traffic lights. The joy of trying to trick a knowledge student with these kinds of questions must be of endless delight to the examiners. The usual routine in working the sheets would be something like, go to school, call the sheet, anything you don't know list it down and organise to see it ASAP. This process is then repeated forever more until you're driving a cab, which could be tens of thousands of times, oh bliss.

Mr Syme versus Mrs Sadlier , Round one.

On the morning of my first ever appearance I felt like I was made of rubber. Nothing could affect me, a bolt of lightning would struggle to hurt me, the sound of general life wasn't being registered. This rubbery, excluded feeling came not through confidence but through shear fear. I woke up that morning in a cold sweat. I struggled to keep down a reasonable breakfast of two slices of toast and three cups of coffee (caffeine, keep alert, get it?) and reports show that I was never more than skipping distance from the toilet. On the morning of any exam you're faced with the old dilemmas of do you try to cram in the last little bit of information, do you rest and trust in the saying that if you don't know it now then you might know it next time or do you fall to your knees, look up, and prey to the god of good fortune and promise an unkeepable promise in return for a score up the carriage office. One thing I would say is that I looked smart. Good suit, nice lilac shirt and matching tie. I looked in the mirror and thought, hold up, maybe I could charm my way through this……'mm, I'd better call those sheets before I leave then, eh? As I pushed my little Dutch onto the road, kick started her up, felt the noise of her purring engine like a tabby cat next to a log fire……alright, I kick started her up and she spluttered like an old fella smoking a pipe but at least we were on our way. With your head inside a helmet, you can hear yourself breathe above the traffic, you can smell your own breath and when you're excited or nervous you can hear your heart pumping from the pulses on your temples. Altogether, the helmet is increasing this feeling of fear like a small amplifier. Horror films are so much less scary if you watch them without sound, obviously as you can't hear the build-up, the drums when the monster is at the door, the screaming when the hero finds the dead housemaid, it's all about the build-up. With a helmet, you have locked in quite a few sounds that are now being amplified and giving you the horror film build up and confirming all you thought, be afraid, be very afraid.

Dutch flew through Seven Sisters at a speed that Milkmen dream of, 32 MPH! got through Stoke Newington with ease and then via Upper Street entered the post code that all Knowledge boys know and fear, N1, Islington or because of the speed restrictions and local council planning, the land of the speed bump. They are everywhere in Islington, even the residents don't like the speed bumps. Sleeping Policemen, they used to be called when I was growing up. God bless Islington council and the numerous car garages that feed off the over eager motorist scraping their spoilers and exhausts over these things. I found a space for Dutch in Donegal Street which runs down the side of the PCO, sorry, Public Carriage Office to give its full name. Parked her up and pulled off my helmet. The sound of my worried heart had disappeared, but I'd just caught a glimpse of my hair in my mirrors, get a comb quickly I thought, or Mrs Sadlier will think the Mark Syme file she has in front of her is the wrong one and will look for the Leo Sayer file instead.

As I walked towards the main entrance to the carriage office, I could see the points collectors outside in the street trying to catch anyone in a suit coming out of the building to grill them about their appearance. 'Excuse me mate, had an appearance?' was the usual start to the bog-standard questions of What stage you on? who did you have? what did they ask you?

At this point, the knowledge boy/girl gets a brief chance to spill all about the last fifteen minutes of their life inside that building, up on the infamous second floor. 'I knew I should have known it, but I lost it and couldn't speak a word' the knowledge boy says as I pass him by, pulling the door open. I thought, they aren't listening mate, all they want is to write down your appearance, get your details and get those sheets filled in. I sometimes think the points collectors should have a psychiatric couch outside on the pavement so you can lie down and give all your stories of woe about your appearance and really clear the air. Can you imagine, 'well, doctor, it all started with the no entry in Ironmonger Lane, it was dark, and I had nowhere to go'. In I went, a nice hello to the people on the reception, be nice to everybody in this building as I need all the help I can get.

As I walked up to the second floor, I see photos of one hundred-year-old cabs and of the development of the trade to the present day, very interesting but where are the toilets because my nerves are asking questions again. Everything in this building says '1970's'. The made to last lino flooring, the bare walls only occasionally decorated with sheets of information or the odd picture of a fella from the 1800's feeding his horse on what looks like an equine taxi rank.

I do, the now usual routine, of making sure that you book in before you do anything. I have sat in that waiting room for up to 20 minutes awaiting my examiner only to realise they don't even know I'm here because I haven't booked in. Out of the booking hall I saw the sign for the toilets and made my way through the door. Pick a cubicle. I shut the door and see the graffiti on the back. One was a drawing of a worn-out face and a speech bubble saying, "is it left, or is it right?", good to see someone has seen some humour in this otherwise Third Reich atmosphere. Wash up and in the waiting room I go. This is the point of no return. I've booked in so they know that Mr Syme has arrived. I take one of the fifteen upright, basic looking, chairs again 70's issue. This waiting room has been the same décor and arrangement for up to thirty years ever since the PCO moved from Lambeth to Islington. That's another great thing about all this, it's the tradition. Nothing, or hardly anything has changed. The way the knowledge is done. The appearances, the fear of the examiner right down to the décor of the dreaded waiting room, everyone knows what it's like once you've been through this system. This place is right up there with Sandringham and Greenwich Naval College.

As I took my seat, I look around me and see another three Knowledge boys. One is sitting upright, back straight as a roman road, eyes fixed full steam ahead, looks like he's getting ready to break ten planks of wood like the Karate

Kid. I'd better not talk to him, or I might be going in my first appearance with a broken arm. The Second one is chewing, yep, I can't believe it, chewing. If he's caught with that in his mouth, he'll be in for the sharp end of an examiners tongue no doubt. Like the guy who turned up in the waiting room once without a tie on, I even shudder as I write this. The examiner swung round the door and bellowed "Mr Thompson?" Yes sir, comes the reply. When the examiner sees his candidate in front of him, he makes no secret of asking the guy in front the whole waiting room, what stage are you on Mr Thompson? 56 days sir comes a quite confident reply. "Well," the examiner says with a sinister smile "Follow me and as we booked you out to come back in 56 days you can tell me whether that will be long enough for you to borrow a tie off of someone". He waited two months for that appearance and now needed to wait another two more, this is temperament testing time. I heard with that story the guy left the building and just stood outside on the pavement for about half an hour in disbelief although he was spotted in Tie Rack soon after.

So, Mr Chewy sat there, legs apart, arms over each chair beside him, he's open to all comers, there's nothing phasing him. If a train rolled through this room right now, Mr Chewy would just salute the driver and look the other way, Mr Chewy made this knowledge look easy. Then I see him. Nervous Nigel. He's sitting there, very cutely waving his hands around like he's directing something. Occasionally I can hear an over exaggerated mumble, "no, leave on left Upper Thames……" then it fizzles out, I don't even get to hear the point he's leaving from or the word street on the end of Upper Thames Street. Now he's got me trying to figure out all the points in Upper Thames Street, he's dragging me down his slippery slope. His Hair has had his hands run through it about twenty times since I've been here. You can see this man survives on a diet of coffee, cigarettes, and his blue book. He looks like walking asbestos, pale skinned with wiry hair and characteristics of a celebrity due for rehab.

One of the unspoken parts of the waiting room is who will your examiner be that day and that's because you don't know. It's all a big mind game. Who will poke there head around that waiting room door and call your name out? Each examiner will have their own character, likes and dislikes, which, as a rumour ridden knowledge boy, you will have known about long before you start appearing. Some examiners like the east end and Shoreditch and all the little, niggly roads around there and some like long directional runs like Arsenal Football club to Fulham football club. Some like west, some like, God forbid, far south. So, when you're sitting there waiting for your name, the pre-exam tension and the mystery surrounding who you're getting is enough to break even the most military of minds. Mr Chewy will call all his questions while sitting on his chair turned around so he's leaning on the back of it like some cocky teddy boy from the 60's. Nervous Nigel? call the funeral directors, he's about to blow. The Karate kid gets called first…. The examiner Mr Wilkins, the east end and niggly road specialist, stands in the doorway and stops for three seconds, so do our hearts, in those brief seconds before a name is called, I must have tried to call the whole of Shoreditch thinking my name was going to fall out of his mouth. "Mr Mahoney?" KK stands to attention in the middle of the room and bellows a parade ground "Sir". One gone three to go. Nervous Nigel, now standing in front of the gigantic map of greater London that presides over the whole room. This enormous map looks at you. You can hear it saying, "come on, have a little look, anything you want to brush up on before you're called?". This is the master of all maps, covered in Perspex and about six-foot square. I'd love to have this map in a room at home, but I haven't a wall big enough and, this one, belongs to the PCO. You can't help at least once getting up and looking on this wall, but you obviously open yourself up to other Knowledge students saying the well-trodden "it's no good looking now, you either know it or you don't".

Now me, Nigel and Mr Chewy all know that we can cross off Mr Wilkins from our feared list. Always nice to cross of the notably hard examiner in the hope of a more forgiving character will lean round the corner with your file. Mr Dixon, ex police officer, very smartly dressed and calm as a disciplined cucumber very quickly utters "Porgie" around the door. Did I hear Porgie ?. I look around and up gets Mr Chewy. I secretly wish to myself his first name is Georgie but surely life couldn't be that good. As Mr Chewy approaches the door to leave the waiting, he takes the gum out of his mouth, throws it in the bin and no one is any the wiser. Pure class, Mr Chewy has this all sewn up. This display of arrogance does no favours whatsoever for Nigel, who is now looking up to the false ceiling in religious pose obviously wishing for that streak of confidence to enter his chemically ridden torso. I'm thinking, Mr Dixon, I've heard he's quite forgiving or at least doesn't think your family catch rats on Jacobs Island if you mess up an appearance, so maybe he's falling into one of the good ones gone list. Nigel had started to carve something in the wood of the chair with his thumb nail. If he gets called before me, I'm going to check it out, there could be a killer in the making with this guy, I could be saving someone's life here. There is a mystery of the unseen smile of Miss Danvers. Like a forgotten city, the legend has it that it is blindingly bright and feels you with ease but, alas, hasn't been seen for an age. In the role of examiner this lady is tough and unforgiving. She is the tension in the waiting room personified. Like all the examiners, very smart but with a look that could make Satan look like a children's entertainer. She swings around the door, and it looks like she is filling every expectation. She isn't happy. "Mr………. Jones". Hold on, my names not Jones. Nervous Nigel leaps up like an addict during cold turkey, "Yes ma'am, madam err miss". He's all over the place. This lack of moral fibre seems to annoy Miss Danvers even more. I fully expect to poke my head around the door to see Nigel lying on the floor in some kind of panic stricken fit with Miss Danvers smacking him around the face shouting "SNAP OUT IT, SNAP OUT OF IT MAN". This is my chance to catch a killer. I lean over towards Nigel's chair and see he's scrawled…. Death to ALL! As soon as I get out of here, I'm on the phone to Scotland Yard. Surely saving the life of an examiner is worth a B. I even feel at one point I may have to check to see if the lady of the forgotten smile is OK because I don't think she's safe if she doesn't score him on his appearance today.

And there I was, all alone. Looking around the waiting room, me, the gigantic map, and a picture of a canal in Venice with a Gondola being pushed along. Benjamin Desraeli was quoted as saying "The Hackney carriage is the Gondola of London". You don't see many TX4 drivers down Park Lane with Punting sticks pushing themselves along, but you can see where he was coming from. For centuries, Londoners have been transported by one means or another by all types of vehicles. It started with the river Thames in times of only one crossing, that of the original London bridge. Watermen and Ferry men would, for a small fee, row you over to the other side of the river where you could enjoy the medieval delights of Southwark. Maybe catch a bear baiting ring in full flow or just enjoy the company of local thieves, scoundrels, and ladies of the night. It's historical fact that the ferrymen would use some extremely colourful, if not aggressive, language enroute from one side to the next with or without passengers. On your journey across the river in one of those small rowing boats you would more likely hear the Ferryman hurl abuse at other ferrymen and their passengers alike. In those days the ferrymen would shout "Oars" or "Sculls" at the top of their voices while drifting along the banks of either side to attract custom and to let passers-by know they were for hire. It's come a long way with the yellow for hire light on top of a cab and continuous regulations forbidding touting. Could you imagine now days, in the vein of the old Watermen, driving through London, hanging out of the window of your cab shouting "East", "I'll go anywhere east". Thank God for civilisation. One of the attributes of this long tradition of Hackney Carriages is camaraderie.

One thing the watermen seemed to overlook in his barrage of abuse of other comrades. It was much more of a dog-eat-dog business back then. Men with horses and carriages did the same job on dry land in those days. Still ferrying people around but with a gentle clip clopping going on. Victorian law still states that a Hackney Carriage driver should always have a bale of hay in the back of his vehicle from those days with horses. I'd love to see main taxi dealers like Mann & Overton or KPM selling the latest TX whatever strewn with hay on the showroom floor.

The horse and carriages made way for the combustion engine vehicles and so on for the last few centuries until we arrive today. Electric windows, iPod plugged into the dash boards, air conditioning, TV's and phones in the back for the punters. We've come an awful long way since sweeping the horse manure up and getting the "Him and Her" couple to the Royal Palace of

Whitehall. Centuries of tradition, struggles and stories and here I am, sitting in a 1970's waiting room where many have trodden before. Where boys came in and went out men. Some of the first knowledge boys to sit in what was this new Islington carriage office waiting room are now retired and I dare say with a few more stories up their sleeves than when they had the last time they sat in my seat. I looked at the Gondola picture and thought of how many Knowledge students have missed the meaning or don't even know the origin of the picture. It would be easy to gaze at this painting briefly and turn away as it holds no great beauty. You'd be forgiven for thinking, yeah, they all painted dodgy pictures in the days when this place was built. Forgiven for thinking anyone who comes up with such soul-destroying décor for a place would obviously think that a picture of an Italian fella giving it large on a river is art. But that is art and life in general, eh? it's never what it seems, and beauty can be in the most unlikely of places. Every time I heard footsteps walk past the waiting room my heart would miss a beat and I'd pucker up, sit straight, and get ready but the minutes went by only adding to my angst. I spotted a penny on the floor, that's handy I thought, let's hope the old saying of find a penny, pick it up, all day long you'll have good luck is true. I bent down to pick it up and suddenly, quietly, unassuming, stealth like, I hear "Mr Syme?". Maaaamm!! My reply is full of nerves and the strange feeling of addressing a woman in such a traditional fashion. She asks me to follow her which I do immediately. In fact, if she asked me to jump through a burning hoop right now, I'd accommodate. As we walk down the corridor, I see names of examiners on doors, names I've had nightmares about staring at me from aluminium door signs. I can only imagine the emotions going on behind those doors. I straighten my tie and attempt to smarten my already acceptable look. A door to the right opens and out comes a smart and firm looking Mr Dixon followed by what seems to be a glum looking Mr Chewy.

Could it be that Mr Chewy got caught out with the Catford one way system? or has he confused the French Embassy in the cul de sac of Albert Gate to that of the Saudi Arabian embassy in Mayfair and driven right through the gate into Hyde Park? All his confidence seems to have been kicked out of him.

He looks pale now. The look resembles that of a spoilt child being told there are no presents. Just as I think God moves in mysterious ways, Mrs Sadlier opens her office door for me. She opened it for me? blimey, I must be new. Usually, I've heard you must do a dam good job in keeping it open after the examiner lets it shut towards you. "Do come and take a seat please Mr Syme" she says with a beguiling smile. The kind of smile that says I can bake the best bread pudding for my family on a Sunday afternoon, but one false move sonny and I'll have you on the floor in a half nelson screaming for your mummy in no time. I take a seat and look round. It's my first time, I need to savour this day, have a good look around, see what kind of stuff is here. On the desk is a cut down podium so the examiner can rest a map of London on.

This is obviously to check how far off the route you're going. Although you can't see the map in front of the examiner it's usually a good idea to use the 'eyebrow test' to see how well you're doing. This comes in the way of while you're calling your route from one point to another, take the occasional look at the examiner's eyebrows. If they seem to have a look of surprise or wonderment about them then it's probably a good time to change direction and take a rethink about crossing three bridges to get to Trafalgar Square. There are two or three maps on the walls. Greater London, motorways, Great Brittan, they're all there so I hope she doesn't ask for South London to Bournemouth. Even if it was on the knowledge, it would take me all day to call it. She flicks open a file with a few bits of paper inside. I see my passport photo clipped to the corner of it. It's my file.

That's the photo I sent in with all my application forms to sign up to all this. It's getting warm in here; has she got the heating on I wonder. "This is your first appearance then? how are you finding it?" she asks. Well, this has started off very civil I think I might come back for another one of these, very amicable I thought. "Very interesting ma'am, I'm enjoying learning it all". She smiles as she looks at me like the villain of a James Bond film knowing her next move will kill me. "Good, take me from the English-Speaking Union to Hamley's toy shop please".

The smile is a distant memory as I look at what now seems to be the Devil incarnate. Her eyes fixed on mine. I'll never be able to do the eyebrow test at this rate, she's too good at the cold stare. Her head didn't even move. Steady, like a bomb defusal expert with the red or blue cable to be cut problem. "Charles Street, Mayfair to Regent Street, ma'am" I replied thinking to myself, I'm now in control of this let's go. Well, if the eyebrow test was anything to go by, at one point they looked like two caterpillars on a trampoline, it wasn't going according to plan. Has she turned the heating up again, I can't believe how hot I am. I thought I'm trying to call over in the jungle here and she's not even offering me water to stay alive. Two or three runs later in various areas North, East, South and West, it was over. "Ok Mr Syme, you haven't scored today" she said regaining the Satanic smile. "There's a long way to go, so keep going and next time you come along, hang your coat up on the coat stand provided in the waiting room". See, if you're dealing with gentlemen, then coat stands are for hanging coats.

Where I come from in Kentish Town, if you left your mother in a waiting room someone would take her and your coat. I didn't mind not scoring as the main thing was that the tense build up, and soul destroying anticipation, was finally over. "Go and book yourself another appointment and we'll see you back here in 56 days". Yippee, I'm free to go. First ever appearance done. Didn't score, didn't expect to. Back past an empty waiting room and into the booking out area. In front of me was a toe tapping, colour back in his face, Nervous Nerris. He'd scored and was displaying the characteristics of triumph. I could hear a little song being mumbled, maybe Anthrax or Black

Sabbath, something dark and deep. Hold on, I know that tune. He turns around to see me and I smile, fearing for my life. Maybe I'm a sacrifice he's going to make in the middle of the booking hall. "I should be so lucky, lucky lucky lucky" he sings gently, as he turns back to book out. Kylie Minouge, surely the world is safe now. "Thanking you kindly" he says to the person booking him out, he's full of the joys of spring now. Me, I'm feeling ok. My first ever appearance is over and now I really feel part of it. I'm given a date 56 days after this one and off I go out onto Penton Street to face the points collectors. I can't wait to start explaining how it all went.

Out onto Penton Street I see the huddle of points collectors. I'm asked by one "had an appearance mate?" ""who did you have?". I like the questions. I feel one of them. We're all in the same boat camaraderie. "Sadlier, 56's". As I explained my full appearance I could see, once the points collectors realised this was my first appearance, their interest faded. I suppose first appearances don't hold much weight. They are either a quick wrap on the knuckles used as an encouragement tool or if the first timer scores there's such a long way to go that getting the champagne out this early would look slightly green of anyone.

Nevertheless, it was great to have my first real chat with a load of Knowledge boys and to catch a few of the other people coming out of the Carriage Office spilling their tales of woe. A woman on 21's came out. She already seemed like she should be driving a cab. I could hear her telling the points collectors about her appearance and then clarifying which bits were worthy of including on the sheet and telling them they may as well leave out the more elementary questions because 'everyone' knows them. Speak for yourself madam.

So that was that. The start, I was now a fully fledge Knowledge Boy. For days after my appearance, I kept thinking it's true what they say about knowing more than you think. With any exam there are elements of self-doubt but with this level of commitment you can't help but know a sizeable amount of your subject. Little did I know, the level of commitment that I was already showing would have to increase tenfold if I were to have any chance of getting through this. One of the great things about doing the Knowledge is that it's all about London. I know that looks obvious but what I mean is that it is a study of a whole city. A very big city. The biggest in Europe and ever since primitive tribes were chased out of town by the arrival of the roman army, history has been being made here. So, furthermore, if you're going to study such a large, busy, overpopulated city such as London you cannot help but start to study life itself. The whole world exists within London. Look around, we've got every nationality of person, language, food, and culture on Earth. You can eat in a different country every night of the year. You can celebrate a different 'new year' whenever they occur and be in the company of the people from those countries when watching any televised sporting event. The popularity of our museums, art galleries and music venues bring the worlds renowned artists to us.

The Knowledge was a gateway to the rich enlightenment of life itself.

I started to view this as something much deeper and what looked like becoming a lifelong interest. While out on my bike, I'd ride around ticking off all the roads and stopping where necessary to mark off another landmark, building or dead-end road etc. While doing this, I'd suddenly find that the certain place where the points sheets would take me would be of great interest if you realised what you were ticking off. I used to love it when I'd realise the reason an examiner is asking Knowledge students if they knew a particular place is because they knew it was of interest and they wanted you to know too. Either that or they just wanted to catch the poor unsuspecting Knowledge boy out and make their life a more miserable place to exist within. I remember standing in Pickering Place, SW1 off St James Street and seeing the Texas Embassy plaque. This was where the state of Texas had their own embassy, and all the paperwork was done when Texas gained independence from Mexico in 1836. I looked around and thought some time ago there must have been Texans coming here on governmental duties, laying down their ten-gallon hats and complaining "my, this sure is a mighty cold place, London, England". I stood there thinking of Texas gaining their independence and these far-off lands and the dusty roads and hilltop gun battles and then I learn that the last duel in England took place right where I am standing. Those were the days, eh? Duels '. Two fellas have a disagreement over something and the next thing you know, they're standing back-to-back with pistols pointing skyward taking ten paces and turning to fire. Right where I am standing, the last duel in England. The same cobbled ground where the blood washed away from the loser and I'm standing on it. See, Johnson was right, it's all here, you've just got to look a little closer. I came out of Pickering Place that day and as I was walking to towards my bike a tall, tanned man looked at me and said in a very deep Texan tone "Hey son, would you be kind enough to tell me where I could find the Texas Embassy?". I couldn't believe it, "it's through there, but it went years ago" I replied. As he walked through the alleyway at the side of the famous Berry Bros. wine merchants I 'saddled up' and drove through Pall Mall East at the side of Trafalgar Square where I saw the well-known Texas Embassy cantina restaurant. Looking back on it, he could've meant that rather than the plaque in Pickering Place. By the look of him, he seemed no stranger to a hearty lunch. This wouldn't be the only time I'd send an unsuspecting tourist in the wrong direction although a little drop of his own history wouldn't have done him any harm. Once I realised that all you have to do with the Knowledge is to be interested in what you're looking at, it started to become a great and, sometimes, exciting hobby.

I loved the way I could start to translate some particularly old, grey subject matters into something interesting and see the tragedy or humour in it all. My days of just going out on my bike learning 50 roads and coming home were starting to become more colourful with my newfound interest. I thought I'd start to go out with a well-planned route to finish my blue book runs and, as a little treat, throw in something of interest to see. I started to see what I was searching for all along, history without corduroy jackets and coffee breathed teachers. If translated into a language you know, understand, and feel comfortable with, anything can be of interest, you just have to colour it in properly.

I've tried to put Dr Johnson's theory to the test by listing places in London that have 'all life can afford'. To see whether you can spend a day in the country, a day on the beach or generally places where you would normally think of outside London to experience. A 'day in the country' could take in far off Hampstead heath and the grandeur of Kenwood house, where they filmed a big scene from the film Notting Hill. Walking around the hills and ponds of Hampstead can take you far enough away from any traffic and, for that matter, people, that you could easily assume you are in a distant part of Somerset or Dorset. Hampstead Village, Flask Walk, Well Walk etc are perfect examples of London being a collection of villages.

Property and roads have stood still in time around there and can help create a blissful walk-through Dickensian London on a wintry evening. The beach? a tough one if you're looking within London although there are certain areas of Putney riverside, where they start the boat race from, that have a decent enough walk down to the river where I have sat with my mate Jeff laughing and joking in the sunshine. You might not get sand in between your toes but the riverside banks of Putney, Chiswick and a different but favourite of mine far out East on the Dockland areas of Wapping and Victoria Docks have expanses of river big enough to create that Sea and horizon feeling.

The feeling of fierce wind blowing in my face while looking out over an expanse of the Thames never fails to fill me with the aura of a Sea captain in charge of his vessel or an explorer from the Middle Ages coming back to port to tell his stories of far-off lands. It's just a shame with these heroic and grand feelings that I'd turn around in full waterproof bike armour and cock my leg over a Honda C90 and chug like a moronic milkman off down the cobbled streets of Wapping, We can all dream, can't we? So, if you look close enough it's all here. Countryside, Beach (well, river). London for sale, River views, very big gardens, close to sixty-eight high streets and one hundred and thirty stations. Must be viewed immediately. The funny thing is that there's a few Russian zillionaires out there that would take that description and offer seriously.

The interest in it all was starting to be a great source of enthusiasm and believe me I needed enthusiasm. Some of the repetition of calling over the blue book runs, and the constant practice of the roads can be mined numbing, so you need to manage the time spent on the real work. Studies show that the brain is at its most powerful for about twenty minutes at a time. Let's hope this is a little longer for professionals such as pilots and Surgeons, eh? Along with my developing interest in London, I still needed to concentrate heavily on getting the real Knowledge work done. I'd plan out my work the night before going out on my bike. This was a very important part of the knowledge. I'd get my big map out on the kitchen table and start to give myself a route that took in all the questions of all the roads and places of interest that were either troubling me or escaping me. As I said before, a few little historic treats and nice places to see coupled with the shady areas of my knowledge would all be included. One of my biggest aims around planning my route was that it would always end up coming back on myself and heading in a homeward direction. The end of the route wasn't always straight, that's impossible all the time but whether I needed to see things in the West End and then in the City I'd maybe throw something in Wapping and the Docklands, so I was still picking up Knowledge while making my way home.

After a while the whole thing consumes you. You can't rest until you know it and when it's impossible to know this whole city road for road and place for place, it becomes an endless search. This is the never-ending road that keeps us all part of it. When you're faced with something in life that must be done, there is no limit to the depths you'll go to get it achieved. You'll rearrange your life; you'll compromise relationships and social occasions all in the tunnelled vision of seeing the light. When the one thing you love, want, or need starts to be detrimental to yourself and those around you, you've got a problem. The chances of your relationship breaking up with a partner while studying the Knowledge are far greatly increased due to the nature of the beast and its unpredictability. You may have excuses for not going to the in-laws, a christening, or the birthday party next Tuesday, but you can always do with a little bit more work on your bike or on the map.

The length of time you remain in this zombie like state is all dependent on how long it takes for you to progress and complete the Knowledge which can be three years, or it could be six, seven, eight. All the time I was planning my routes and cracking away with all that was being asked up the carriage office I was never calling the questions sheets. I was more learning the set routes and progressed to big, long directional routes like those of football stadium to football stadium. Believe me, Arsenal football club, in those days in Avenell Road, Highbury to pre-Russian Chelsea football club on the Fulham Road is a dam long way to go on a Honda C90 but it really does start to give you a feel of how big London is.

One of the things they say about doing the Knowledge is that the more you know London the smaller it becomes. When you start to know what is around every corner and where every street leads to, it not only feels smaller, but it also feels like home. You are out on your bike so much that you start to live on the road. You use the local shops in whatever area you happen to be in when you need a drink or something to eat. You stop off in a café to get something warm inside you to set you up for the rest of your day. You need to occasionally visit a toilet out there and that can mean visiting all sorts of places just for that reason alone, Hotels, pubs, Petrol stations, coffee shops all become places you've visited in these areas you're getting to know. By the time you've completed your Knowledge you've probably had a first-hand experience of the vast majority of local amenities so it comes as little surprise when a suit from the City asks "Could you take me to Clapham High St. on the corner of Mr Clarks hardware and perfumery shop?"

Time was ticking by, and my next appearance would soon be looming. As always, head down work hard but I had to start really testing myself by calling these question sheets. This involved getting the question sheets from a Knowledge school. Getting the sheet home or with a call over partner and just starting to call from one place to the next. Every road name and, hopefully in a straight line from one place to the next. This is the true test of what you know. This is the absolute number one thing that will show you if you are progressing with your Knowledge. The proof of the pudding is in the eating. I realised all too late that it's no good just knowing your favourite one hundred runs and hoping for the examiner to ask you anything like these you must be able to do it 'freestyle'. The word 'freestyle' has never been used in connection with the Knowledge but it's the best way to describe the coming away from the regimented set routes of the Blue Book and directional runs. The old saying of 'can you call it' really comes into its own here. If I was to call the gherkin to the London Eye from point to point, I'd better know how to do it and in a reasonable way as there is no such Blue Book run or fixed route going across town for me to memorise, it's all about the seeing.

The appearance sheets were now becoming my main priority. Not just for the stark realisation that I didn't know where I was going but also to keep abreast of the constantly changing names of places. Nightclubs are one of the most regularly changed names followed closely by Theatre shows and hotel chains. From a dusty rock to a diamond, eh? In fact, after a while the mentality should be developed where you welcome mistakes because these are the holes that need filling before you present yourself to your examiner.

The Chinese have a saying when the student is ready the teacher appears. I now started to concentrate on the time this was all taking and started to do the worst thing a Knowledge boy can do, and that's predict when they will get their badge and be 'out'. This is the spiral of darkness in Knowledge boy world. How can you enter predictions of something that is historically known for being unpredictable, madness. This is a path to self-destruction as all your hope and dreams of climbing this mountain will start to chip away at you and add an insurmountable pressure on you. With your family, friends and relatives already putting up with a zombie like figure roaming around the streets of London the last thing they need is for you to be is all doom and gloom. Everything will be affected. Clarity of study, concentration, and a general happiness, and I know, as I was that unhappy soldier. Don't predict I told myself, I wrapped myself in a love for the subject and the journey rather than the outcome. I'll never give up I thought. I may never get my badge, but I would have had a dam good and interesting time trying to get. I had thoughts like these coming up to my second ever appearance, little did I know, I had a rollercoaster of a journey just about to begin.

Mr Syme versus Mr Thomas

Smart, very well groomed, and extremely straight walking. Almost glowing with confidence. Mr Thomas, Ex police officer and now public carriage office examiner. The kind of man you see sometimes being interviewed just as a silhouette in SAS documentaries. Your initial thoughts are, he's not very big but I get a feeling that this man has hardly ever come second in any situation. As you look further into the eyes of such determination you realise the feelings you now have are pure and simple…fear. I'd stepped up my bike work, I'd been calling more regularly, and I'd now taken the decision that the full map of London should be on hand every second of the day. I was thinking that with the amount of effort I was now putting in that just three points from these 56 days appearance would start this new phase of work off with a bang. It would prove to me that I was now doing the right amount of work like some of those guys who have scored in every one of their first four appearances, they knew the amount of work they were doing was sufficient to get their badge, I, on the other hand, didn't know my arse from my elbow. I was sure this could be my chance to score my first three points.

The night before my appearance with Mr Thomas I'd been watching a documentary on interrogation. This was all I needed to fuel my inner fear of my imminent meeting. Mr Thomas would've been out running with a gas oven on his back, getting in shape for the morning, while I sat in front of the TV thinking of how Pizza and fear could be an explosive combination. The documentary went on to explain one of the methods of interrogation was to have you in a room with two doors. One door would be just access into another room while the other door would be a steep drop to the street below. While being interrogated, you would be blindfolded, dragged around the room and then the blindfold would be briefly ripped off to show you the drop. You'd be asked questions and threatened with being thrown to what you've just seen. Silence to all the questions would lead you to being dragged up off your feet again, ran around the room with the blindfold on to create disorientation and then thrown out of what you believe is the street below but alas, is just the door to the next room. I didn't need to see these scary tactics to know that if the PCO could enforce such measures they'd certainly think about it for some of the pricklier candidates.

That night, after calling over a heap load of runs and some of the more cunning back routes I slept like a baby. I was up all-night crying and wanting comfort. As the sun crept through my bedroom window, I saw a strange cloud formation. I rubbed my eyes and there in the blue sky I saw what seemed to be the number 3 and the letters PTS to the right. It was a sign. I was on course for three points this morning. Up, shaved, smartly dressed and a small bottle of cheap champagne on ice to celebrate my scoring. On went my helmet, kicked started Dutch and away we went. The journey down to the Carriage office in the morning rush hour traffic could serve as a handy distraction before an appearance. On any vehicle smaller than three men standing side by side you take your life into your hands. Rush hour traffic is sometimes quite unforgiving. For once, not just one or two people have somewhere to get to in a hurry, everyone has. You can feel the tension in the air. Even on my little Honda, people think twice about giving way or allowing a little extra space for me to creep through. People are different in their vehicles. I'm sure I've seen one man taking a bend while reloading his fishing catapult in case of any driving disputes on the other side of the bend. The language is usually colourful and unfortunately not far away when someone disagrees with someone else's thoughtless behaviour. The renowned neurologist Sigmund Freud had a theory that we don't like in others what we don't like about ourselves. If you look at road rage as a behavioural thing Mr Freud, had it bang on. On the road we see greed, panic, and are often in situations that create a lack of spatial awareness. If you had in-town rush hour traffic as a friend, would you invite them to dinner at your house?

Now that my stress levels were at a high, I pulled into Donegal Street N1 and just about squeezed my bike on the end of the Motorcycle parking bay. Islington Borough council are notorious for fines and tickets with parking misdemeanours, so I had to budge a couple of bikes up by hand. I jumped off my bike and began taking off my waterproof bike trousers and jacket.

Off came my trainers and out of my top box came a neatly folded tie and pair of shoes. That reminds me of my mate Jeff who used to follow the same procedure although he used to use his brother's wedding suit and a pair of regulation postman shoes for his 'smart' look at appearances. We'd always joke about him walking into the booking hall at the carriage office with the said wedding suit on and still having the carnation pinned to the lapel. Booking in with a load of confetti all over the floor would help to lighten the atmosphere in there I must say. Once ready and tie straightened, I sauntered up the road trying to take it all in my stride once again. Seeing the points collectors gathered outside and other Knowledge boys either going in or coming out starts to get the heart pumping and your body temperature rises. I walked past one Knowledge boy talking to a points collector only to hear the collector saying "Well, he's not easy that Mr Thomas". That was it, I thought someone was going to have to help me open the door as I went weak, and everything started to go dreamy. 'You alright mate?' one of the other knowledge boys enquired. "Yeah, nervous, you know, appearance and all that". He looked sympathetic. The kind of look that says you're walking into your death, but I can't do anything about it. A nod of heads and we finished our exchange. I booked in and went and took a seat in, the still undecorated, waiting room. I think they have been meaning to put a lick of paint in this place for years but something else always gets in the way. Down I sat with a whole waiting room full of knowledge boys and one girl. The girl looked over to me with a kind smile. I smiled back which made me feel at ease. The nervous tension and occasional testosterone fuelled comment from one of the knowledge boys just stirred feelings of needing motherly comfort. It was all very Freudian at this stage but, as previously said, anything to take away the nasty man mummy. . Names were being called and bums were leaving seats. At one point Mrs Sadlier poked her head around the corner. I thought, seeing as we've met before, she would have showed out, a little wave or something. Not even a wink. She doesn't call, she doesn't write. Alas, it seems she sees more than just me in a month. Then, cat like with commando style cunning,

Mr Thomas appeared at the waiting room door. "let's have look, who we got here" he said while gazing down at his scribbled list of knowledge candidates. "Mr………." he deliberated. I knew it had to be me as I'd lived up to that moment with the continual confusion of how to pronounce my surname name. "is it Mr 'Simm?" "Syme Sir" I replied in a solider like fashion with my now straight back and my arm almost rising to salute. "Come on then" he said with already a hint of despondency. As I followed him down the grey corridor to his office, I looked either side of me and saw there were the names on the doors of examiners that I'd yet to have. Names that filled me with fear and names that I'd heard various tales from previously seen knowledge boys. The following continued in a left right fashion, you know, military style. A left, a left, a left right left. Just as I was thinking about rolling in to his office and shouting out 'cover me, I'm going in' we arrived at his door. After being told to come in and grab a seat, I gave the room a quick glance over to get an idea of what kind of person I was up against. I noticed everything was in it's place. Pencils were newly sharpened as seeming to be part of an ongoing maintenance drill. Three or four panoramic pictures of London bridges and obviously a giant size map of London which would be behind me as I sat down. Then I noticed the main picture behind Mr Thomas's head. Almost professional in it's taking. A framed photograph of him on a gravelled driveway with a brand new, silver coloured TX2 taxi. Alongside the cab was a sports car also silver coloured parked in a V like way where the noses were almost touching. The owner, Mr Thomas, standing proudly in the middle of both vehicles wearing sunglasses and black leather driving gloves. Let me just say that again. Wearing black leather driving gloves. Within a second this picture conjured up thoughts of famous black leather glove wearers of merit. The villainous James Bond character Odd Job sprang to mind leading me to quickly search around the room for a discarded bowler hat. But one image stuck there. Steve McQueen, Bullet. I thought. play this clever. Buy him a grey polo neck jumper and maybe a picture of the undulating streets of San Francisco and bingo, 3 points in the bag. "Take me from the old Vic theatre to the young Vic theatre". No messing around, he went straight in with a tricky one. The Old and young Vic theatres are about one hundred feet away from each other in The Cut SE1. The problem being is that without being allowed to do a U-turn under knowledge appearance rules, this turns out to be a tougher question than first seems. Up to the roundabout at Waterloo station and back down the ramp, along The Cut and set down on the left. He seemed OK with it, but you can never tell until the end when they give you your 'obituary' speech. "What about the Mermaid Theatre to Aldgate East station". I know this I thought. Sometimes, when you sit there under all this pressure, you see the light. A perfect line going from the first to last destination. I called out the whole route in about fifteen seconds. Along Upper Thames Street, Mansell Street round to the right and, ta daaa, there's your station sir. Things seemed to be going well. I ran another run a bit scrappy but passable in my eyes and then came the last one. "Name every possible left turn off of Oxford Street travelling from West to East". Wallop, he'd just been cleaning his gun up until this point. This was a proper question. It comes away from the calling a route mind set and places a more overall feel to your knowledge appearance. In the early stages of your Knowledge, it can take some getting used to which way you are travelling around the city due to the turns of the river and planning of one-way sections etc. A great example of this is the trick question of when travelling over Westminster bridge from Big Ben in which direction are you going. Well, with you being able to see the City on your left and looking over the bridge virtually at Elephant and Castle you're not left with too much to do as it is definitely not North. It turns out to be East solely due to the massive turn in the river Thames at that point. On the map of London, knowledge boys often refer to this point as the elbow.

West Oxford Street? my mind now racing. I could feel my proverbial fingertips hanging on to this appearance. He looked at me straight in the eyes and said, "you do know which end your starting from don't you?". I bumbled around and finally blurted out Tottenham court road sir? in the hope that I'd literally guessed right. No chance. He'd seen this before. A wounded animal trying to fight out of a desperate corner. A sigh of disappointment from him told me all I needed to know. He flicked through my file on his desk and scribbled something down. After a brief second, he handed back my point scoring card and just said "you've got a long way to go but this is only your second appearance, work harder". I stood up from my chair, took my card back and said thank you. I didn't need to look at my card straight away to know that it said D, no score. As I walked through to the booking out area, I looked at my card and D, confirmed. As a lot of appearances end in very few words being spoken. Unless they tell you that you haven't scored, you hope to look at that card and find a C has been written there. Hope springs eternal. I was feeling gutted. The subject that I put so much effort into was bashing me in the face and I was starting to feel despondent. Despondency is one of the worst things that happens during the Knowledge. It's despondency that keeps you from ploughing straight back into the work and it keeps you off your bike. Optimism and enthusiasm need to be held onto throughout the Knowledge, but these can be as slippery as an Eel to keep when the D's start coming one after another.

Mr Syme versus??

Worse things have happened at sea. Two appearances and no score yet. Although it was just my first two appearances of which the first one you don't expect anything from anyway, it's the tick tock factor that starts to creep in. Looking at it, the last four months on the knowledge I hadn't progressed at all. I'd started to get closer to going backwards. On each level of the Knowledge, you have seven appearances to score four times. Taking two away from seven was leaving me with only five appearances to score four times. Percentage wise, I had an eighty percent pass rate to achieve in those left. Going on the past two, there was cause for concern in my work rate.

Life would have to change. More work needed to be done but not just that, I needed to understand London. I would have to feel that this was truly 'my place'. Although I would try to call over as much as possible, you never feel like you've done enough. Sometimes just before bed I'd just quickly have one last look at that Catford one way system, nothing too intense just a little glance, well, it was bedtime. While out pointing I started to read up on the places I was sitting outside. Not all of them but the more interesting ones. Oceanic house on the corner of Pall Mall east near Trafalgar Square, this is where tickets for the Titanic were purchased. The subject of so many stories and films, part of a more current history and you stand outside feeling like the tickets could almost still be bought through those doors. Schools realise that getting the kids interested in these subjects means going to the places, feeling it, smelling it, touching the materials, being around what you're talking about. This plan of familiarising myself with 'my place' started to work. Although marvellously enjoyable, it was hindering some of the more productive work that needed to be done but as the Buddhists say, it's not the destination but the journey that matters. Listing out my work for the day I would put little Asterix's next to the more interesting of points. The café on the corner of Burdett and East India dock road that the carriage office asked for the previous day wouldn't really get a second glance, although you'd have to see it. The old Sail making factory a hundred yards along would get a good looking and a 'read up'. Making one-hundred-foot sails for the clippers on their way back out of the East and West India docks to bring back twenty tons of tea from India. After taking a month to pick and harvest and fight the Ocean and fend off pirates the sails made around East London would be instrumental in making sure that we all have a nice cup of Cha. I was becoming a proper little know it all. I was calling well, and Dutch was running well. I still looked like I hadn't seen enough winters but nevertheless, I felt I was progressing. Surely, when I go up this time, it's time to score. The night before my ten o'clock appearance I made sure that every single run in my Blue book was called, all four hundred of 'em !. I'd taken down the map of London and laid it across the dining room table. At one point I thought I'd spotted a strangely shaped road that didn't seem to register with a certain part of

Southwest London but then noticed it was a crinkle cut oven chip making its way west along Cremourne road in Chelsea. As always, the night before any exam, get to bed early. Again, as always, the night before any exam, you won't be able to sleep until midway through dawn.

Getting ready, I felt shattered. I know, I thought, I'll take the tube to Angle. I'll let the train take the strain while I relax and maybe run over a few last niggling questions. Suited and booted I marched briskly down to the tube station and……. first train ten minutes. Ten minutes is like an eternity on the tube. The crowds build up and the tension rises. You start to judge on who you'll be able to get ahead of either through strength or cunning. Little old lady? she'll be cunning with age, but she's lost the strength, she'll come second in my race. The big fella with the barbed wire tattoo and the goatee beard, he'll get on through strength and, as his look says he may be politically conscious and a general thinker, maybe cunning as well, he's one to watch. As the train pulled in, we all went to work employing our own techniques of boarding. The big guy took a deep breath, surely not a last minute hesitation. Now's my chance, during the big fella's inhale, I board like an Amazon python, one fluid movement. I go to take a seat but, on my shoulder, the little old lady uses all the tricks a woman of her age has found over the years. First, I get the bad back walk and then the Werther's original sweets are dropped on the floor followed by a faint cry of disappointment. I must help and in doing so am then obliged to offer my seat. She knows she's won the train boarding challenge. Me and the big guy will have to be content with each other's arms pits for the next sixteen stops.

The change onto the northern line brings another delay. I just can't get on the train. The passengers on these commuter trains are professionals. They purposely keep the space to a minimum. There's not a gap left, I haven't got a chance, it'll have to be the next train. I look at my watch and I have fifteen minutes to make the appearance. It's always preferable to be early but this time, I'm cutting it fine. I finally get on the train, more armpits and more excuse Me's but I'm on. A delay in the tunnel, this surely means I'll arrive about the time I'm meant to be called. I run out of Angle station. Straight up White Lion Street, no time for the leisurely walk-through chapel market today. To run in a suit could be the worst idea anyone could have but often people in suits have appointments to keep and are forced into running to keep them. I reach the main doors, points collectors outside consoling and joking. I show my appointment card and the lady at the reception clicks the door for me to enter to race up the stairs to the second floor. Nowhere else in that building matters but the second floor. Card out, I jump to the booking in window. There, fresh faced, is a younger guy that I haven't seen before. He smiles and I hand him the card knowing that I'm a few minutes late, but the waiting room looks busy from what I saw so it won't be a problem slipping me in. "Oh, I think, 'erm…. you may be too late" he says with all the conviction of someone who's done a job for about four minutes. I apologise and say that I thought I was never going to make it, trying to wrap my excuses in humour and light conversation. "Let me just check" he says like I'm trying to get into the White House with a ticking sound coming from my inside pocket. "Yep, it looks like you've gone past our seven-minute ruling". Let me just say this loud and clear to myself…SEVEN MINUTE F****ING RULING. I haven't scored in four months. I have just endured the journey from hell. I am now sweating from head to toe which will soon turn into a very manly smell and they tell me there's a seven minute late ruling. Why not ten or eleven or make it nine and three quarters. "Sorry, I couldn't control it" I said but this was futile. Talking to the old British Empire, pre-programmed, rules are rules, admin clerk, was a waste of time. Obviously, I could only imagine what happens now. The way a system like this works never allows for a bending of the rules. It was with this thought that I knew my fate. A system like this wouldn't allow a pat on the shoulder and rearranged appearance for ASAP. I'm on a cycle, a fifty-six-day cycle. I just couldn't believe they would do it. They did. The young clerk checked with his superior and it was confirmed. My next appearance would be in fifty-six days' time. This Appearance would go down as N/A. It would be four months since my last appearance. It will have taken me eight months to score once if I was successful on this next appearance. Most of a year and still no nearer to my goal. The amount of discipline it took not to take down the Carriage office brick by brick that day is a skill. The cloud that started to appear in my life at that precise time was enormous. To say a mild form a depression is not overly far from the truth. A vocation you have chosen, a challenge that you have come too far, a future that you consistently talk of all held in limbo. I needed a release. Psychologists' say that shaving off all your hair after particularly gloomy times in your life is symbolic of a fresh start and moving on. Although I kept my hair, I did think of something I'd seen on programmes concerning mental health before. Exercise, and lots of it. The feeling of sweating, and breaking out of your normal head space, would be welcomely therapeutic. Therefore, I decided to run over every bridge in London. Tower bridge to Kew bridge. I know, I was losing it but at least I was trying to get it back.

Twenty-one miles of bridges

I once cycled from Walthamstow to Brighton, the seaside. I thought this bike ride constituted as the famous London to Brighton cycle run but without the fanfare and ribbon round your neck at the end. I found out later that the London to Brighton cycle ride usually starts about ten miles further into London than where I was and usually already on the main road down to the coast. My error of distance would soon make itself fully known on the bottom end of the A23 when, so exhausted, I threw the old rattler I was riding into the hedges and decided to hitch hike the rest of the way. Unfortunately, the hitch-hiking idea didn't work out. Nobody accepted my thumb and I had to swallow my childish anger and fish the dam bike out of the hedges.

Back on the bike with a backside that looked like it had been on a Nando's grill, I saw a sign for Brighton. Thank the Lord I thought until my eyes glanced to the right and saw it said ten miles. My word I had to find muscles, strength, and stamina from somewhere to get me down there. I'd looked up and saw that this long stretch of road had no lighting and thought that if I didn't get a move on this place will be the darkest patch on earth at sundown. With no lights and a bike that had two gears, stop and slow, I wouldn't have a chance. There would be beasts in those hedges that David Attenborough would be interested in seeing but would scare the living daylights out of an athletic chancer like me. I suppose it didn't help me wearing two pairs of jogging bottoms and a jumper over my two t-shirts. I thought that going at speed on my bike I would encounter wind chill. Wind chill? where did I get that from? I must have stayed up too late one night watching rock climbing on one of the satellite channels, wind chill, God help me.

You can tell I wasn't used to this kind of thing and was obviously only doing this ride to fill an otherwise average Sunday afternoon. Like the misjudgement of distance to the coast, wearing all this clothing also caught up with me as when I started out that morning about half past ten, it was a gloriously sunny day and zero wind, I should have known. By the time the bike went skyward into those hedges on the A23 I think I'd lost half a stone and could see an oasis of water. Of course, it was no mirage, it was the sea, and it was Brighton…. ten miles away….as the sign said.

I reached Brighton bedraggled, didn't even go down to the seafront. Basically, due to the sheer physical exhaustion I suffered on my virtually Essex to Brighton bike ride, I rode from Blackhorse Road tube station to Brighton railway station. Once on the train back to Victoria, I leant my bike against my legs and gazed out of the window and was overcome with an enormous sense of achievement. Looking back on it, I'd made that Sunday a day to remember for the rest of my life. I made an adventure for myself. Albeit just for a day, I'd made something out of nothing, and it brought with it fun, challenge, excitement and despair, a lot more than trying to guess how much the Ming vase was worth on Antiques road show.

I've always been a fan of these programmes, where the presenter gets to go around the world and show us the sights and sounds of the globe. I've also been jealous of the fact that they get to bang on about how much of a good time their having. The viewer is left looking around there living room thinking of what shirt to wear for work the following day with no hope of getting to these wonderful far-flung places, unless you've got nine grand sitting on the sideboard. I would sit and watch these programmes, daydreaming of the opportunity to have a nine-month expedition around southeast Asia while gloating to the rest of the nation of what a right little tickle I've had. I suppose a film crew, itinerary planners, and fully funded trips, while being paid handsomely, with the added promise of book and publishing rights, are just so hard to come by don't you think? If I hear one more TV presenter say the word 'amazing' when watching tribes eat with their hands or doing a 'vlog' at half five in the morning after sleeping in a tent, I'll need taking away from the public.

Walthamstow to Brighton was all the excitement I could muster that day, but it was free and a different idea than going to the local for lunch. I loved it. I'd proved to myself that I could make life a little more colourful than usual and these were the seeds that were to raise their heads again in my current time of gloom. Obviously when I came up with the bridges run idea, I didn't know the distance. I didn't know the route and if truth be told, I didn't know how many bridges cross the Thames within the radius of the Knowledge. I had literally invented this fun run for myself. I'd checked with the internet, there didn't seem to be any other official 'bridge running' club. I thought the best thing to do as planning went, was to get to know the course. Although by now, I could call every road from Tower Bridge to Kew, the course would differ slightly as I'd be able to run certain parts that didn't include roads such as the Thames walkways. Even during the planning of the route with the full map of London on the table I'd started to feel better.

I was enjoying looking at the map. At some points I was discovering what life was like without the continual burden of the Knowledge. No need to be concerned that I wasn't doing enough. No success or failure at the end. It was exciting. I'd drawn the route over my laminated map and written down the amount of mileage old Dutch had done up until then to know how many I'd driven at the end and therefore know roughly the course distance. I basically planned my route out like I was going to go out on my bike for the Knowledge that day.

Back at the Bank where I worked on the 'Island' of Canary Wharf, I'd been promoting my route to colleagues. I even had the self-promoting idea of approaching one of the local newspapers, The Wharf, to publicise my 'crazy' run. I spoke to a very friendly Journalists there and he loved it. 'We'll send a couple of guys down to see you, you know, get some pics' he said all very journo like. We also arranged an 'interview' over the phone at home. I remember being at home putting some insulation in the loft and answering the phone to hear that it's the newspapers. I laughed to myself, thinking how many interviews had been done in a old dust ridden loft. I gave the reporter my reasons as just for fun, that I love London and, over the past couple of years, have become hooked on jogging, which wasn't far from the truth, and thought it would be a great thing to do. I didn't say that I was studying the Knowledge and through pure desperation needed to get some colour in my life.

I could hear muted excitement from the journo down the phone. Almost like he was thinking this is great, something to get my teeth into. No more cats up trees for this paper oh no, now I've got my own Eddie the Eagle right here at The Wharf. The plan was they would do the Article over the phone but when the time came to get down to Tower bridge, they would send a photographer and he would follow me on my run taking shots of London and my sweaty red face. He would follow in a car sampling the delights of London's sandwich shops and newsagents while I pulled my illuminous legs along the embankment.

Mileage, check, waterproof clothes, check, Oil for Dutch, well it looks dark in there, so she'll be alright. I drove Dutch over the whole course. Zig zagging up and down, north to south. It was great. I was looking forward to running what I was riding.

Along the way I was checking where I could forsake the road for a more leisurely riverside run. Southwest was where most of the water views away from the road were. Stretches between Chelsea, Albert and Battersea looked like they were well trodden joggers' routes anyway, so I'd be part of the crowd there…. Jogging incognito you could say. Finishing on my bike at Kew bridge, I'd got a real feel for the bend of the river and at some points, like Waterloo bridge, you could see most of London laid out in front of you. This was all very helpful for my Knowledge as well.

I'd taken my original mileage away from my current mileage and saw that it was about twenty-three miles. With the riverside walks and corners being cut as legs don't need to do one-way systems, I roughly saw the route as about twenty-one miles. This was long enough for a bit of fun and as I said, I made the run up, every bridge East to West in a north to south fashion, so I could call it what I want.

After all the preparation, shorts, bottle of water I had a dilemma. For bits and pieces, I needed to carry on the day i.e., money, keys, mobile phone do I purchase the belted pouch commonly known as the Bum Bag. This was a dilemma as I'd grown to know these horrific additions to fashion as the type of accessory that only European tourists carry around and very efficient German fathers. I couldn't get away from it. They were handy little things. I couldn't jog this run with a rucksack. I couldn't take a carrier bag around with me, that would just look too no frills and a leather satchel was out of the question. No, I would have to embrace the efficient German father look. I had an idea though. I would fasten it slightly higher around my waist and therefore could pull my t-shirt over it saving some street cred at least.

The following week I left work, as usual, on the Friday night to best wishes from friends and colleagues at work. The newspaper confirmed their man would be on Tower bridge at eight in the morning. There was no way back. People now knew I was taking this on. I now had to go through with it. That night I drank only water. Plenty of pasta like the marathon runners before the big race. I got the tube down to Tower Hill in my jogging gear of shorts, light waterproof jacket and……. Bum Bag………. covered, secret. I met the photographer. He wanted a couple of pictures of me stretching before the big run. He wanted my leg up on the bridge wall with a view of Canary Wharf in the background as the sun was coming up from the east. It was a great idea, but I looked at my legs and thought these aren't made of plasticine. I finally got my leg up on the wall and the pictures were taken. It looked like I knew what I was doing but I think that was my first stretch since I'd taken off my school blazer. Nevertheless, I agreed with the photographer that we would keep in touch along the route by mobile phone. He would ring me and ask how long it would be until I reach my next bridge then scoot round in his air-conditioned Daimler with the heating fully on and snap a couple more photos enroute. As I set off, I saw him walk towards s 1976 Datsun with an ashtray on the dashboard. It was most probably warmer and cleaner being out on the road than stuck on bridges in that old thing.

I was running. Pace yourself I thought. Think Tortoises and Hare. The views were terrific. As there are so many joggers along the Thames nobody knew what I was taking on. I suppose it's a little bit different when you have twenty-six thousand other joggers with you during the London Marathon but, hey ho, I was pleased with the obscurity. The weather was sunny and warm. I was keeping in touch with my photographer and every time I spoke to him, I knew I was doing well as he started to predict the next bridge and was a couple behind. Looking back on it, I don't think it would have taken an overly fit person to run faster than his old Datsun anyway but his surprise at hearing on which bridge was next, was encouraging.

For that time jogging through London, the Knowledge was a thing a the past. A dark cloud, an unwelcome friend that I didn't have with me that day. The endorphins were kicking in and I felt great. The occasional kick of the heals as I leapt over various road works and litter obstructions gave me the feeling of achievement, something I hadn't felt at all on my time on the Knowledge. After you get over the initial stretching of the muscles and aches and pains you can fall into a rhythm running where you don't know you're jogging. I looked around and was enjoying it. I saw a puff of smoke as I approached Hammersmith bridge and knew that the Datsun was catching up. The riverside along Chiswick and Thames Road is picturesque and, again, something that made the run easy. Over Chiswick bridge and I'd be north of the river with only Kew to go south over to finish. As I ran over Kew bridge, I knew that I'd done this in just under four hours. I was pleased. I didn't think of the time at all but on seeing I'd done it in under four hours I was well pleased. I was greeted at the finish by a smiling photographer with a camera worth more than his car. After a few photos next to the sign stating you're now in the borough of Richmond upon Thames, I shook the guy's hand, politely refused an offer of a lift back somewhere and walked northwards towards Kew station. 'Hey Mark, what's that at the side there' he said squinting. I looked down, look back up and replied, 'a Bum Bag'. The secret was one we'd keep although I would keep a close eye on the forthcoming article in the local rag.

I felt better. My head was clear, and thoughts of Tibetan communes were fading fast. I would come back to the Knowledge empowered. Organise my work, plough through it and be victorious. Well, it sounded good anyway.

Syme versus Price

Nice price they called him. A real gentle, seemingly wise, old man. The suits he wore bore the resemblance of a1960's civil servant. On reflection, Mr Price was the epitome of the public carriage office. The grey suit and mahogany rimmed glasses were all he needed to get the job done. He behaved kind and gentle not for the fact that he was weak in any way shape or form more in the way that he had literally seen it all before. This man didn't need to shout about his experience in the London cab trade. He didn't need to come across as someone who had an over exaggerated political view. This man was the experience. He was the cab trade. It was like he had been dipped in a vat of liquid entitled 'LONDON'. As you never know who you'll get on your appearance I took no chances. My work rate had trebled. I was now calling over the blue book daily, well about one hundred runs a day. I was extending my time out on the bike at weekends by taking it more seriously and getting up at the crack of dawn....seven'ish. My head was clear and through my full-face helmet I knew I was seeing a lot more. I was getting home at night knowing that I'd ticked off another fifty points of interest and some of the more obscure ones that the examiners had been asking for. It's also common practice to take a good look at those one or two roads and one-way systems that are still not getting into your brain. As all the practical work on the bike is an all-year-round thing., you're obviously subject to all the changes of the seasons and the occasional clement weather surprise.

I remember once having to tick off on my list of points to see the church of Saint Magnus the Martyr on Lower Thames Street. One examiner had asked it and I, like all the other knowledge boys, raced out to make sure we knew it as life was one big imminent appearance. I was always of the view that no point the Carriage Office had asked for is, pardon the pun, pointless. You always found in the end that there was a reason. Whether historically or socially, there would be a valid reason to know the point asked although Lidl supermarket on Burdett Road over in the east could only be of interest if you were searching around for the cheapest German frankfurters.

Magnus the Martyr, Lower Thames Street. A Church that throughout history had undergone many a rebuilding and alteration. It had Been through the plague and partially destroyed during the great fire of 1666 and through all this the one thing that got me on my bike to tick this one off was the 'lump of wood'. In the courtyard of the church stands a great big piece of timber. Railway sleeper looking, this piece of wood has had a perimeter put around it by the church and a brass plaque stating that it is one of the oldest pieces of wood in London and therefore Britain. It was found to be part of a Roman wharf although more romantically some have said maybe even part of the original London Bridge. The very bridge that was the only path crossing of the Thames for about one hundred years. The London bridge that was lined with houses and shops precariously hanging on the edges. The medieval marketplace that was the setting for the demise of Nancy in Charles Dickens Oliver Twist. 'Nancy's steps' are on the southside, Montague close, under the current bridge with a blue plaque stating the fact. It's only with the benefit of knowing the background of what I was seeing and taking an interest in the stories behind it all that made that piece of wood so marvellous to see.

Over the course of time there have been four London Bridges, but this piece of timber could have been from the very first one and I'm touching it with my beaten, not so waterproof, motorbike gloves.

I saw on the T.V once that inside the Fishmongers Hall, on London Bridge just above this church, they have a throne like chair carved of wood from two or three of the past bridges. I'll have to get in there one day to look, all I have to do is find a registered fishmonger. Again, standing in the courtyard of that church, taking time to realise where I was and what had gone before was just one of those confirmations in life that you're pleased that you stuck by something.

I'd ticked it off and kick started 'Dutch' into action. I noticed that since my arrival in the courtyard the rain had been consistent. Lower Thames Street was swimming in rain. There's was no traffic about as I scootered towards the traffic lights just missing the amber and slowing to stop for the red when what can only be described as the noise a jumbo jet makes just before taking off came hurtling towards me from behind my helmet. I swung my head around and there, in an old Ford Granada, that obviously had no previous careful owners, was a little old lady with eyes full of fear spinning a complete circle in the road. She had obviously thought otherwise of the amber to red combination at the lights and, as the City of London is notorious for its traffic cameras, decided to slam the anchors on. As I watched her almost ballet like spin towards me, I gripped the handlebars and thought this is it, I'm on my way to the top of the bridge without using any petrol. She finally came to a harrowing stop, side on to the lights. Looking straight at me in the left-hand lane, she had just completed a massive 540 degree turn to no rapturous applause. Just a soaked knowledge boy on a mud splattered Honda C-90. If that stunt would have been attempted at the annual Clapham Common freestyle festival, she would have been crowned queen of the half pipe and given some kind of hip hop b-boy chant. I suppose that's the way it goes. Loads of unsung heroes and miracles happening all around us to no applause. To me though, she'll always be that queen of the infamous St Magnus the Martyr spin.

Later that very same day I was heading home after getting the majority of what I set out to do with the rain finally winning the battle of the day. Soaked through, socks ringing wet and the drips from my visor going down my jumper onto my chest, I took a little corner in the Finsbury Park area a bit too sharp and didn't see the manhole cover in the road and off I came. No real damage to me or the bike just a bit of embarrassment. Luckily my helmet was a full face one so all the public can see is this soaked, yeti like creature scrabbling around in the road looking for a black topped ignition key on a black tarred road covered in four-inch-deep puddles, oh what joy.

The weeks went by, and appearance day finally came. I needed to score on this one or I would face the dreaded 'red line'. Being red lined is when the examiner has no other choice but to draw a line underneath your past failed appearances and requires you to start again on a new set of appearances. This is always a big kick as you know then that you had just been given a longer time to get your knowledge done. If I could score on this one, then I would then have a very tough time in trying to score on the next three after that but at least I won't have to start 56 days again. This was the fourth out of a possible seven appearances at 56 and I sat in the waiting room of the carriage office with the face of a death row inmate. Pale and lifeless I sat waiting as the names were called out. 'Hargreaves' bellowed an examiner and up got a tall guy with a very short moustache. There was a load of comic material in this guy but today wasn't the day. I wasn't in a positive mood. 'Smith' called Mrs Sadlier. That's one of the good ones gone I thought although I didn't even bother playing the game of who I was going to get as I was now entering a meditative state like those who walk over hot burning coals and feel no pain. Then, as I sat, I smelt the comfortable smell of warmth coupled with wool. Maybe a faint hint of an open fireplace with empty sherry glasses. In the doorway with a halo hanging around the top of his head stood Mr Price. Nice price. Slowly I watched as he mouthed the words 'Mr Syme'. Thank the lord. I could expect some real traditional knowledge here. Manor house station to Gibson square. Victoria station to Grosvenor square. This man knew that nobody hardly ever asks for Mohamed Al-Fayed's shop rather than saying 'Harrods please'. He knew that the public were people like me and him and that cab rides, and routes, are a continual balancing of views and opinions and to find a stringent technical point to it all was a game for accountants and scientists……and madmen.

I followed him into his office and took a seat as asked. He was wearing a cardigan under his suit jacket. A cardigan under a suit jacket? I could have hugged him. I sat looking at him as he ruffled my file and looked at my track record. I was hoping he would tap his knee and offer a granddad like story or maybe some hot milk before we started but that was just me comfort finding. He started off easy. Waterloo station to Euston station. A straight line to get me started with too massive places end to end lovely. Then it warmed up. The Shakes at Victoria to The Pasha night club which is about ten yards to your left from where you are, but you have no left or right to get anywhere and thereby forcing you to drive in an elaborate circle half the way around SW1. Then I just couldn't place Spring Street W2. My word, one of the most common places to drop passengers off for Paddington station and I don't even know where it is. On this form he must have thought it's OK going from

North to south with this guy but if I want to get to somerset in the southwest by train I'm better off walking. The walls were crumbling. Mr Price continued looking for one last glimmer of hope. Kenwood House, Hampstead. Here we go I thought, if this goes anywhere but back into town I may as well offer him money, or this appearance is lost. To Muswell Hill Broadway. That's it. The assassin had found his man.

The red pen was draw from the highland tweed breast pocket of his cardigan and the line was draw with a small ruler for precision. To be fair he was very explanatory on what he thought, and it was all very encouraging. It was kind of strange. He had just told me that the past ten months appearances had come to an end and that the hill was getting steeper but the way he delivered the news made me feel comfortable. It was the kind of feeling blues singers seem to have. All the aggression and frustration had gone, and I was just left with my little bike and my blue book and a heap load of old point sheets to get back into tomorrow. That was the end of my first lot of 56-day appearances. To a lot of knowledge boys, to mention 'first lot' they wouldn't know what you were talking about as the knowledge to them was a full-time, full-on procedure and the stages came and went. For me, and lots of other part timers, life gets in the way. You try to juggle all the downs of the knowledge with a little bit of real life as well. You still try to be sociable, go out and maybe laugh once in a while but you know your forcibly trying to get a life as there is something draining you and that's called The Knowledge.

Yeah, I was down but I'd given so much that there was no way back. I was downtrodden but I would get the map out and try to make it more interesting, work smarter and try to look at myself and my methods in various ways………. then I'd buy a harmonica and play it as the sun went down sitting on my window ledge occasionally moaning something bluesy like 'mmm oh yeah'.

DEJA VU

The time, as usual, was flying by. My first appearance of this new lot of 56 days was in about a weeks' time. For a little bit of a fresh approach, I thought I'd do some directional routes in the way of all the football grounds in London. East to west, west to south, north to west. These runs send you everywhere and because of the location of the football grounds they take an awfully long time to ride on a moped. Possibly the longest one you get to ride is Arsenal to Chelsea. For this one, it's helpful to pack a lunch. The bike must be filled up with petrol and it's preferable if you phone loved ones halfway just to inform them, you're OK. One amazing thing about this run though is that although Chelsea is in Southwest London it doesn't cross the Thames, no bridges are taken and therefore, as a firm North Londoner, you don't have to…. Gulp! go South. I'm sure that any cab driver who lives at the back of Peckham Rye sitting on the rank at Paddington at eleven o'clock at night being approached by a passenger asking to be taken to Nunhead would want to get out and hug the person for taking them all the way home. I like going south, always liked a bit of water, love a bridge, as you know, and there are some lovely little gems to be found over there. Look at Bermondsey. Taking a little ride up Mill Street just off the top of Jamaica road you enter the land of Dickens and Oliver Twist. It is up Mill Street that the squalid and filthy downtrodden area of Jacobs Island sat. An Island, as all around it was murky water running alive with rats and human waste. This is where the Villain Bill Sykes not only lived in the Charles Dickens tale of Oliver Twist but also hung on for dear life in the final scenes of the film from rope strung across the Wharf buildings. Poor old Bill, down he went to the baying crowd below and all this just off Jamaica Road. That area of Bermondsey alone has had many a book filled with its former dark past.

On a lighter note, the famed actor and right old Londoner Sir Michael Caine was born just down a bit off Lower Road, in what is now Ann Moss way. Of course, the road didn't exist at that time but it's on the site of the nursing home and there's a blue plaque up to commemorate the fact that his mother pushed and gave birth to a right cracker who would go on to make such classic films as Alfie, the iconic Italian Job, and Dirty rotten scoundrels. Ok reserve judgement on that last one.

Back to trying to find Chelsea Football club. You can't help thinking that no wonder Chelsea have always had this tag for being a fashionable club. Just riding around Fulham and the Kings Road, I think of the days when this was really swinging sixties London. There must have been no better time to be into a football club in those heady days when everyone tried with fashion and the football weren't bad either. Strolling up Kings Road surrounded by guys in the latest of Mod wear and the occasional dandy looking fella with a velvet jacket and silk handkerchief hanging from the top pocket. Accidentally bumping into three miniskirts, bob haired, high boot wearing models on their way to a fashion shoot involving a few Mini Coopers and an umbrella could possibly be one of the great ways to go and see the impending clash at Stamford Bridge.

When you hear of millions of pounds being earned in the City and all these highly paid careers or antique dealers wheeling and dealing you never really see the back end of it. How it's spent, how these people live with all that wealth. Well, as you make your way through Knightsbridge, and the royal borough of Kensington and Chelsea you see how it's spent and how it's lived. The latest models of luxury cars, houses that seem to be bigger than your local supermarket. Everybody has got three or four shopping bags from the highest of couture fashion when, added up, comes to a fortune spent in one afternoon. I know that at one point, the convenience store to the wealthy, Harrods, were offering a deal where, if you spent more than ten thousand pounds in one trip, you would get a forty-inch plasma TV set. This resulted in all the chauffeurs outside Harrods constantly loading TV sets into the back of Mercedes, Rolls Royce's etc. It was comical to see. They may as well come out into the middle of Knightsbridge and give the TV's away as anyone who has just spent a lot more than the ten thousand usually has quite a nice TV anyway. From my average working-class background this place seemed like toy town. Money is never an issue. I often wonder the freedom the mind has if the worry of money and having everything secured since birth has never been there.

I stop on my bike to have a little lunch, well, I'm in the 'royal borough' so I may as well do as everyone else and have a spot of lunch. As I fish out one of my corned beef and piccalilli sandwiches, I see that after making it so far in my top box the sandwich has an imprint of one of my few bike spanners ratting around in the back. It doesn't feel the same watching people suck the froth off a tall latte with a crab and rocket sandwich in hand as I eat what seems like an imprint pad from a key maker. One thing I notice about such an affluent area as I stand next to 'Dutch' is the smell of cologne. The wealth is tangible to the nose. Everyone is so well groom around here that the volume of Perfume and aftershave being worn has quite literally filled the air. This run really takes it all in and on these big journeys, with practice and calling it over religiously, you really do get a fill for the villages of London.

I found myself on Earls court road. If you go way back in time, apart from being fields, gardens and vegetable patches, this area was also part of the ancient manor of Kensington although, as time has got on, you wouldn't blame anyone for thinking it is now the modern-day manor of the Australian outback and crocodile creek as the area is now so well known for antipodeans. In fact, I think Earls Court Road was generally called Kangaroo Alley for many years. The influx of Australians and New Zealanders to Earls court was one of those natural word of mouth things that just happen. There are many examples of this in London and one of the biggest is China town where the people make it the town. Nothing is planned and things just bump and push and somehow come together to create these wonderfully exciting places. A town planners' nightmare you might say. Organised chaos, but it has always worked.

I get onto the Fulham Road and another few hundred yards find myself outside the main gates of Stamford Bridge. As I said earlier with the fashionable Kings Road and the buzz of a time when everybody was trying new things I look up at the main gates and think of another fashionable time of the 1980's when I used to get over the Arsenal. Sergio Tachini tracksuits, every kind of Adidas trainer, desert boots, waffle trousers, this time was my swinging sixties and for those years in the mid-eighties, clothes, music and football was engulfing the streets and media. I look around Fulham Broadway to pick up a few points like the Blue Elephant Thai restaurant that has always been top of every Knowledge boy's list and look over to the White Hart pub. The scene of many 80's football violence stories and the exaggerated and, often, not so exaggerated fables of the Chelsea head-hunters staving off attack from all the other well organised, and equally headline making, football gangs of the day.

A little peep round the corner leads me and Dutch into North End Road market, the more affordable side to Fulham. A mix of true Chelsea fans like stall holders Jamie and Terry on the fruit and veg along to my great mate Chris in the betting shop. I'm glad my helmet is full faced as if I'm spotted in the market I'll be forced to stop in Chris's shop for tea and must listen to Jamie ribbing me about how Chelsea run all over Highbury ten years ago.

I evade detection and turn around to head back. It's now about one o'clock in the afternoon on a Saturday. Chelsea are away which has made this trip do 'able. Chelsea at home would have been a no no. Anyway, one o'clock isn't bad going but now I had to make it back to Walthamstow which is where I lived at this point in my knowledge. Looking at it on the tube map sends a shiver down my spine. Home is a place far far away, where birds tweet and sunsets warm the heart. Ok, maybe Walthamstow isn't exactly like this but the occasional gangster rap tune from twelve guys sitting on a wall all wearing their hats sideways can be equally mellowing if you know everyone.

Back I go, the wind has started to pick up which makes the bike move all over the place. The trouble with these little Hondas is that one good gust of wind can knock you off and you never know where you'll be when it happens. It can happen turning into a small quite square surrounded by houses or more scarily it can happen pushing thirty along the Victoria Embankment with the slight feel of rain in the air and a skip lorry eagerly trying to make it home.

One big gust of wind in these circumstances and you could find yourself looking at very large nuts and bolts of that said lorry. You must stop at the side of the road if the wind gets too much as continuing becomes a hazard not only to you but other drivers. The last thing they want to do on their way home is scrape a pair of waterproof bike trousers from their tyres. About two hours later I find myself home, thawing out. As there is so much to take in on these directional runs it's quite often the case that after half an hour of being home you forget where the hell you've been all day. I sit down with a cup of tea and flick through the football runs especially the Arsenal Chelsea run and some things start to fall into place. I suddenly realise easier links from Islington to the west end and how the West End can go west into Hyde Park and Knightsbridge. Hey, things are sinking in, this new set of 56's maybe a good chance to try some different things but, more particularly, start a sticky list of things that are giving me problems and ironing those out…. right, number one, the missus……only joking.

Is it Sir, Mr or just Courtney?

As I understand it, his name is Courtney although I, and many others caught in the headlights, called him Mr Courtney. See, it's the conditioning. You get so used to giving unconditional respect to anyone associated with the Public Carriage Office that even when given the opportunity to call someone by their first name you still resort to Mr. A great big West Indian Rastafarian, Courtney was the shining light that would brighten the dreary grey corridors of the Carriage Office. Big, got to be six four and, as the song goes, broader than Broadway. This man knew his London and still actively worked his cab on the days he wasn't examining the likes of me. You knew that you would be in for a little bit of Southwest London when faced with Courtney. He has made it public that he loves the whole cab driver testing system in London and is thankful of his completion of the knowledge all those years ago when he worked it out on the tables of the Clapham Manor Street school. He is a big supporter of the cab fraternity. You'll often hear his views on London radio stations when the time permits. With masses of dreadlocked hair and an unmistakable West Indian accent, Courtney was such an outlandish breath of fresh air to have bellowing out the names in the waiting room, I thought it would be great to have an appearance with him when I was in a more controlling position. Right now, I just wanted to be tested by one of the disinterested admin staff lingering behind those booking in and out windows, but I knew that wish wasn't going to be granted. My direction was now progressing at great speed. I was linking Islington with Chelsea and how Chelsea can become Battersea and Battersea could even lead me to Putney although I'd have to take a deep breath on that one. All these southwestern areas of London couldn't be further from home in Walthamstow. I used to look around some of these areas and think to myself, Trinity Road SW17? I'm a long way from home here my old son.

I would occasionally look at the tube map on the back of my London A-Z map book and run my finger from say East Putney station to Blackhorse Road station at the top of the Victoria line and think going back a hundred years I'd be in bandit country here, fields and cows would have been my biggest obstacle not the Swandon Way gyratory. My word, the roundabout at Swandon way in Wandsworth is a big boring lump, although the aroma of the nearby Ram brewery and all those hops and that yeast being stirred up can take away some of the greyness. Direction was my main aim right now. I started more confidently pointing in the direction I needed for any route. I wanted to hone this little trick as it would serve me well in an appearance. When you are asked the starting point of a run up the Carriage Office there is a very brief chance for your brain to scowl the immediate area knowing how to exit from all angles before the examiner asks the destination point. I thought I'd give myself a great chance by knowing all exit points within a split second and thereby be ready for the next point already half ran in my mind……it was a plan.

Blue book as the staple and the long football directional runs were really helping. The test of pointing in the right direction could be done at home. I would say to myself, 'I'm standing on Euston Road and Judd Street, now where is Stoke Newington'? that way! my finger would go up and point through fifty buildings to Stoke Newington somewhere. It was quite a cool game to play after a while. I would be watching Local London news on the T.V and try to call the immediate roads in any one news clip. I'd be wishing for reports in areas where my knowledge was a bit sketchy just so I could brush up on them. With some parts of Walthamstow being known to be a little less salubrious than some parts of Kensington, and with my little 'Dutch' being my prized possession, and the only thing that was currently getting me around London, I was naturally concerned for her welfare. I therefore decided and, looking back on this looks crazy, to keep 'Dutch' in the back garden of my little house off Forest Road E17. The problem with this security conscious idea was that to get to the back garden you had to enter through the front door and go through the hallway, past the stairs and through the kitchen to the back door. Not so bad on foot, like normal people, but to see a soaked Knowledge boy turn up and the front door mysteriously opened, by a, not altogether convinced, but very understanding partner, was a sight for the eyes. Apart from exhaust fumes in the house and the sound of an engine flying past your roast potatoes in the oven there was a problem on entering the house on 'Dutch'. Being an old Victorian terraced, there was a step from the pavement onto my small front garden and an even bigger step going from the nicely tiled walkway through the front door into the house. This required a Hollywood style rev and ride up to achieve the momentum needed to make certain of both steps.

I imagine sometimes, as I'd arrive home from some far-off London borough, that I'd be greeted by cheering crowds on both sides of my road. As I got closer the chanting would start….'Go Marky, Go Marky' and then I'd treat them to one or two revs on the bike. The youngsters would be impressed and cheer louder, jostling for a better position as they knew from past entrances that when the revving starts 'he's getting ready for take-off'. Looking back, it must of looked bizarre seeing a motorbike being driven into a house but I really did feel comfortable having Dutch in the house rather than chained up for the semi-professional joy riders to disappear off into the sunset, or at least, to the other side of Tottenham. I do remember once, my neighbours, looking on with wide eyes, how me and Dutch entered the house. With the front door wide open I'd give Dutch a few revs and, with one quick twist of the throttle, go riding straight through the hallway into the kitchen and out to the garden.

It was an early appearance, my first one back. Starting afresh on 56's gave a sense a renewed hope. I could be a different person on this set. Confident, knowing much like Jules Vern's character Phileas Fogg when he travelled the world in eighty days, never hurried always calm. Nope, not a chance. Nervous as hell as I arrived. Boom, a great big, 'Right then, where is this Mr Syme'. Courtney. I've got him. This is going to be a very expressive appearance so I can relax caring for the usual straight tie dilemma. This one will be just about what I know. We both sat down, and he said, 'let me ask you something sir'

Gulp, this is going to be personal. 'You ever be out in the West End on a Saturday night?' he starts with a wry smile. 'Erm, yes sir, a few times' came my reply. 'Well then, take me from the English National Opera to the Astoria'. Yep, no right turn at the end of St Martins Lane but shouldn't be a problem popping out of Covent Garden, it's in the bag. Next one, "now then, a lot of trains come into Paddington and some of those passengers have never even been to London before". I expected the stories off Pricey, but not the big guy. "I get into your cab, and I want you to take me to five of the top tourist attractions within reasonable distance" he finished and lent back on his chair. I cracked them out, Buck House, Big Ben, Trafalgar Square, The House of Commons and onto the London Eye. It was a straight line, and no chances were being taken and he knew it. He might as well have a flip chart of all the pictures of those attractions on as he knew I'd go for those especially from Paddington, who wouldn't. The appearance became quite enjoyable, he took it easy on me. Looking at my file, he must have thought I deserve a break, and this was it. 'Ok' he said as if offering no other advice which was different to most of my appearances. He handed back my card and said, 'you are off and running Mr Syme, take it easy my man'. He was cool. Like meeting a Quentin Tarantino character, stylish, cool, with oodles of street cred. More importantly…. I'd scored. Three points. Nine to go and I'd be on 28's. My word there was no stopping me now. If there is anything more egotistical than a clean and brushed up knowledge boy who's just scored I have yet to meet it. There is nothing anyone can tell you about London when it has just been confirmed to you from one of your superiors that you do know what you're talking about, and all that time spent has just been recognised as a true path with a clear ending. I think I'll be having peppercorn sauce with my celebratory dinner tonight and oh, make the Blue Sapphire gin a gentleman's measure will you my kind sir? Life was certainly looking up.

A day of being nosey

There is nothing like a ray of light to fill the heart with hope. Spirituality was pouring over me. I understood that when you have just the shirt on your back that hope, and the realisation of a brighter day are the most powerful of feelings. I gave Dutch a good cleaning. Checked my waterproof clothing. Made sure I had comfortable clothing underneath and even stuffed my top box with a healthy-looking lunch. When I say heathy, I mean in volume not necessarily carrots and lettuce. Today's work would be an enjoyable list of points that I just wanted to see. I wanted to stop outside every one of these places. Have a little read up on what I was looking at and take the time to reflect on what a great place this city is. I'd start by riding down Lea Bridge Road, across Hackney and Whitechapel to the Docklands.

What a place Docklands is. I've read that in its heyday, being one of the biggest loading ports in Europe, if not the world, that just on the Isle of dogs alone there were over one hundred and thirty pubs. One on every corner some of the older residences have said. Serving over one hundred thousand dockers. You think it's busy now with the financial population scurrying all over 'The Island' but it's only a third of what used to inhabit this place. The noise on busy days must have been immense. From loaders to porters, ship hands to sailing crew, every one of them men. If you look around the modern Docklands today with its high-rise glass monsters and slick suit wearing new residents you would think you've walked into the future. Everything covered somehow in shiny chrome facades and new, kept immaculate, tarmacked roads. This new look town has a place but what got me on my bike was the glory of it's past. When those guys got home at night after such a hard day on and off ships, in and out of those enormous warehouses, they were tired, and I mean tired. With hands like shovels, moving coffee arrived from Brazil in rough woven bags, then unloading the latest produce from north Africa, lemons and limes spilling all over the wharf, the hustle and bustle must have been exhilarating. Old dockers have been interviewed in days gone past and they have said of times back in the 1930's when not only West India quay but all along the Thames it was so crammed with ships and boats that you could walk, from bank to bank, across the Thames, jumping from boat to boat and never fear of falling in the drink. Looking at all those, now redundant, cranes that line the well-kept walkways of new housing, always gives me a melancholy feeling. The laughs that must have been had sharing such a tough but interesting time must have been fantastic. At the end of a gruelling fourteen-hour day dealing with all manner of nationalities to then all fall into the nearest pub to drink the night away must have been like scenes that only filmmakers could imitate. The young porter who usually works the boxes of limes from Grand Canaria being made fun of by the more experienced Dockers over the fact that today he got the job of moving the Robusta coffee beans from Rio de Janeiro. He now stands in the pub, covered in coffee dust looking like a miner while a group of Russian sailors look on not knowing the language but find his darkened look as funny as his friends.

The development of Canary Wharf gets its name from the connection to the North African Canary Islands from which many an exotic fruit had been shipped to our shores right into the heart of London. With the East India company controlling every item going in and out of those docks there wasn't much room for 'a little extra' shall we say. Although there have been tales of East London families going back to the early 1900's enjoying Mango and Melon breakfasts and sitting around in Limehouse basin basking in the summer sun with a large glass of Caribbean Rum which had made its way across the oceans and onto the dock and, as luck would have it, fallen into the lunch box of a hard-working docker to 'look after' for a while. I'm in awe of the place. I'm fascinated by the people. Talking of the people and the controlling administration of the East India company, like many authorities, there came a time when they had to seriously look at security for 'The Island'. As with most large ports, Liverpool docks coming to mind, there was a need for an extremely large wall to be built around the area and thereby, hopefully, keeping the black-market scoundrels away from the incoming merchandise. With the employment of a few hundred bricklayers, the East India company commissioned 'The Wall' to be built around the Island. This wall stood the test of time. Keeping out many an unwanted visitor. From the opening of the official East India company docks in 1904 right up to the late 1970's 'The Wall' gave the Isle of dogs a closed community feel. Some say insular. I once heard an old lady from East Ferry Road commenting on the new developing area say the sentence 'It was better when they had the bloody wall up' confirming that the locals took some comfort in being 'locked' away from outsiders. The bygone generations of the old Island are extremely few now although I did stop on my bike near the East India pier in Pier Road and got talking to a lovely old fella who had never, and I repeat, never left the Isle of Dogs, he was eighty-nine years old. Mind you, some of the pretention I've seen in places like Kensington and Chelsea, he's better off where he was.

As I travelled around the docklands, I thought about my knowledge and couldn't help but think that this 'nosey day' could only help my progress as I would have positive associations with my points and places and thereby taking away the feeling of work. I wanted to stop riding around for a bit and crack open my top box for a bit of lunch. I looked at a few of the off shoots along the outer peninsula of the Island in the form of Manchester Road. I saw David's Square and all those wonderful looking swish flats, or should I say apartments to keep the new investors happy. I took a little ride along Saunderness road and round the back of The Isle of Dogs police station.

I stopped at the top of Glenariff road outside the Watermans arms pub. An unassuming little local with a couple of hanging baskets that looked like they could do with a little more attention than the landlord was giving them. The pub is nothing glamorous itself but, again, if you know what you're looking at, it's a whole different story. This is the pub used in the iconic gangster classic The Long Good Friday in which Bob Hoskins plays Harry Shand the notorious London gangster and every London schoolboy grew up watching in the mid-eighties. In the film, the pub was called The Governor General and was the scene of the IRA bombing towards Shand. An absolute classic of a film and strangely enough all about Shand's efforts to develop what was then a very baron and desolate Docklands. If Mr Shand could see this place now. On the back of The Long Good Friday, with the foresight of the development of the Isle of Dogs, some have cheekily said that maybe a gangster or two may have wanted their hands on the developing contracts but what with all the Investment Banks now residing here that maybe there is a shadier form of villain behind those global empires. It's not for me to say but with all the trouble those banks caused in the run up to the 2008/9 recession maybe we would have been better off leaving it to the likes of Harry Shand and his band of broken-nosed brothers.

I left the Watermans arms after looking down the slip path where the Poplar rowing club glides into the Thames and headed off for where the sandwiches where to be eaten, Burrells Wharf. It is here that the great engineer Isambard Kingdom Brunel launched the very much awaited first sail of his greatest design, the SS Great Eastern, the biggest ship in the world. At over two hundred metres long, twice as long as the Monument to the great fire or twice as long as two Big Bens laying end to end, it was a monster. Taking so long to complete, and with many fatalities in the construction, she finally slipped off the launch timbers in 1858. It could travel from here in E14 to India without having to stop to refuel, something unheard of in those days. The crying shame of this masterful feat of engineering was that not only did Brunel die a few days after her initial floating but, in the end, she couldn't keep up with the new and faster ships that were being made in those day and making trips from here to India and America became financially unviable to keep going. I sat on an old piece of the, original, timber eating my sandwiches. With little old Dutch sitting beside me, I was thinking of that famous launch day, Brunel would have stood at the top of this slope with his big old cigar, and designer top hat, watching his creation slowly, amongst a thousand shouts and screams, slip into the water with one of those great big honks of a departing ship. Laughing to myself that there is no way I'd have had a chance to sit on this wooden slat on that day but today, bright, and sunny, dressed like an unfashionable spaceman, I get the chance.

Burrells Wharf is a marvellous place with a terrific view across the Thames.

The 'apartments' look like lovely places to spend your Sunday mornings reading the papers, gazing across the glistening river. It would be an absolute crime if any of those fortunate residents didn't know of the history and grandeur of the Great Eastern and the mossy timber that lay beneath the railings of their balconies. I was starting to feel that I should have many more 'nosey days' in the coming good weather. This was helping my Knowledge no end. Not only did I feel I was starting to know this place but in some way, I felt I had an emotional attachment to the area, a shared experience if you will. My fascination with boats probably means I was a mariner in a past life, although anyone could think Pirate or drunken sailor would more likely fit the bill. I can't really swim that well if not at all, so, if I were to have been a mariner in a past life, I don't think it ended too well nevertheless it's an interest that has led me to some wonderful views and lovely afternoons out with friends along riversides and Wharfs. The word Wharf, said to stand as an acronym for WareHouse At River Front was proven to be a load of nonsense. That said, I want proper, set-in stone proof of this, as I love that and I'm sticking by it.

Mr Syme versus Mr Jenkins

Mr Jenkins. Sort of the earth, Working London cab driver. He's out there more than the Knowledge students. He's out there so much it's been rumoured that if you buy a postcard of any part of London, he's on it somewhere. For once, in the whole mystery of my Knowledge appearances, I knew I was going to have Mr Jenkins when I went up next. I was fiddling about with my score card when I noticed faint pencil marking on the top which had been badly rubbed out. I made out the coded scribble as Mr J-56. I worked it out that, although I'd never had him before, that it was about time I did as he was being quite busy with appearances lately and heard that he was a straight-talking nice guy. A sprightly 50-year-old I'd say. A good head of silver to grey hair, quite wavy, good comfortable clothing, and a walk on him that said he was no stranger to romance and the odd night on the tiles. The rumours were that he would waste no time in using some more colourful language but wasn't in the slightest bit aggressive with it. More jokey than anything. Some of the other Knowledge boys who'd been up to see him said that all the humorous swearing and shouting he'd get through would have a strangely calming effect on the person in the chair as it was rather like being up the Knowledge school with your mates ribbing you about another route where you've crossed the river more times than a ferryman.

I parked in Donegal Street, on the free for motorbike bays, alongside the Carriage office. I had about half an hour to spare so took my time getting my bike gear off and transforming into a smart Knowledge boy. I would think nothing of getting undressed and slipping on trousers and shoes and knotting a tie while standing next to my bike in the middle of the street. All that mattered was the imminent appearance.

Another fella began parking up next to me. I thought I'd strike up a little chat as this could help both of us with our pre-test nerves. His name was Carl and there wasn't a thing he didn't know or so he thought. As we chatted, he popped a cigarette into his mouth like he was just about to throw me up on his knee and tell me all about life. 'Ah, I see you went for the standard Honda C-90 to get all this done' he started. 'I get a lot of work done on this Yamaha 125; I get round to see so much more than your average Knowledge boy'. I started to look at Dutch and think he might be right, apart from drifting around side roads, we're only good for pizza delivery. Even that we might have to knock the occasional pound off for late arrival. Carl came from Croydon, so I was already classing him as a non-Londoner and something of a strange out of town alien which is obviously unfair, but I needed something in my locker to tame this wild beast. He said he went out on his bike every night after his lifeguard job at the local pool. I imagined Carl strutting around the deep end with his speedos on with his whistle at the ready, it was just the perfect job for him. 'If someone wants saving, I'm in like a fish, believe me, they're more than grateful afterwards and the odd phone number can be prized from the pretty ladies once they've dried off'. I was starting to feel sick. Carl was in a land where only him and David Hasselhoff inhabit. I thought I'd steer him off 'Carl mania' and get some Knowledge chat in. 'd'you know I can never get my head round those turn arounds over there in Catford' I threw in waiting for superman to give his view. 'What the old Brownhill,

Sangley and Plassy to get you right back onto Catford high street'. Ok, he knew his stuff, but a little humility wouldn't have gone amiss. Looks like Carl was off that day when they taught those meanings at school. 'Yeah, you see, it's all about being part of the area' Carl said, as if the person standing in front of him wasn't following the same path. As Carl flicked his cigarette right across the road I thought, just for something extra about the Knowledge, I'd just say about the new no entry from Great Portland Street into Devonshire Street which used to be a great way of staying underneath Marylebone Road but now was one way coming at you for that part of Devonshire Street. It was like I'd just given Carl news of a death in his family. His hands started to shake. I could see his complexion changing a darker shade of red. He reached for his cigarettes. I thought this would be a good time for me to gently slip off. I reached the top of the road and took a sneaky glance over my shoulder. Carl was head down into his A-Z on the seat of his bike with what looked like two cigarettes on the go. Looks like the mighty fell for those brief few moments and little 'ol me felt slightly pleased to have been the David of this Goliath.

In the waiting room were the usual suspects. A nervous one, or all of us I should say, a flash one chewing gum with his arms spread across two chairs. A silent, but tough looking, tattooed guy who looked like he was on day release just to get this appearance out of the way. Sitting there worrying, or mentally trying to escape, I was woken by the bellowing sound of Mr Wilkins, the East London and Shoreditch king, calling out Miss Walnut. With that, Mr Wilkins left the doorway and headed off to his office leaving the waiting room looking at a petite blonde girl get up and head off after him. Just as she was about to leave us all, she turned around, and in the foulest and gruffest voice to be heard this side of Billingsgate fish market said, 'that's all I need, this geezer to ruining my day, as if my piles weren't bad enough'. Whoa, looks can be very deceiving I thought as I looked at Mr A wing across the room noting that his nose was turned up like a disapproving cleaner who's just spotted what state the family bathroom is in.

Before we all had chance to have the fishwife's forum Mr Jenkins appeared round the door. Silence from us and silence from him. 'Right, who have I got' he said as he looked at his slip of paper. 'Someone good I hope' as if I wasn't nervous enough now, he's giving me a drum roll to leave the waiting room. 'Mr Syme?' he looked down his glasses to see me standing up. 'Sir' I said, thinking this is a man who's going to like a little respect and, hopefully, present me with the coveted three points I richly deserve. 'Come on then Bonzo, let see what you've got'. This man was already class. As I followed him down the hallway, I couldn't help but think, with his flowing grey hair and well-kept skin, that this man had musician written all over him. I mean, he looked a bit like Eric Clapton. As we entered his office, I was starting to hum Wonderful Tonight. With a blink of the eye, he said 'Eric Clapton, it's on him Slow hand album. 'Sorry sir' not even thinking what he's talking about. 'Wonderful Tonight, the song you're humming, it's on Eric Clapton's Slow hand album, so good they released it a year later as a single and the rest is history'. My mouth could have touched the floor. This was one of those times when you meet someone who really does know everything. Unlike Carl, with these people, there is no way out, you're already picking up the bronze medal. 'Let's hope it's a wonderful night in the Syme house tonight then' he said, getting straight down to business with the map on his desk mounted podium. 'Fifteen Penton Street (The Public carriage office no less) to the Wellington Arch please and don't hang about' he said in a cockney tone. That's the thing about these appearances, just when you think you might be on for a little light conversation and the musical history of someone like Eric Clapton, you're pushed right back into your seat and your brain must get into gear because they know they've led you in now and lulled you into the false sense of security. I finished the run and straight away he said, 'if you wanna go that way fine, but I'd like to see that for less than nineteen quid on the meter'. I didn't know what to say. I'd never worked a meter. I didn't know how a meter calculated the fare. All I knew was that in my head I'm now standing in the middle of Hyde Park Corner. 'Do you like Pie and Mash?' he said. I thought phew, he's giving me a bit a relaxation time to get ready for the new run. 'Yes sir, with liquor sir it's lovely' I replied thinking he's going to get the biscuits out in a minute, and we can have a game of darts about lunchtime. 'Kelly's in the Roman then, to Manzes, on the other side of Tower Bridge, it's not that far'. He said it like he was already fed up with today's work and most of all, fed up with me.

As I was calling the line out all I could here was Mr Jenkins tutting and mumbling things like 'cor blimey' and 'what round there?'. I finished the run, even with all his heckling. It's at this point in every appearance that you quickly flick back through what you've run over the past fifteen minutes and try to judge whether you're on for three points or not. 'Right' he started, 'your knowledge is awful'. 'You know it's awful, you're messing about with silly little roads trying to impress me, and not only are you f***ing it all up, but you're making it harder for yourself'. His tone was so honest, and the odd expletive, really drummed it home.

They say that Slang is the language that rolls up its sleeves and gets on with the work. When you hear it, there's no prancing about, it's straight on the money, and there's no getting away from it. He had me. I thought I'd throw in a couple of sneaky ones like Victoria Park Square and Clare Street off Bethnal green road, but I was all over the place thinking I knew it but just digging a bigger hole. 'Now I can see from your history that you're progressing so I'm going to give you a little incentive, don't ask me why, I must be mad or drunk, but seeing as the pubs aren't open yet, I must be mad'. He finished talking by handing me back my card saying' Now go on, p*** off and book out and, for Christ's sake, learn these roads will ya?'. I thought, hold on, this sounds like he's kicking me up the backside but also giving me three points. I shut his door and walked towards the booking hall. Looking down at my card and, quite clearly, there they were, three marvellous points. Actual tears welled in my eyes. I'd done a lot of work this time round and Mr Jenkins knew it. This was the first time I'd scored twice in a row and couldn't be happier. I could see the benefit of facing different characters up the Carriage office and Mr Jenkins proved admirable in his judgement. I booked out and flew out of the carriage office to face a hoard of points collectors. I felt like one of those Hollywood actors when they exit the limo onto the red carpet only to be surrounded by paparazzi taking photos and asking questions. Except it was raining, I was wearing my work suit which had more shines than a French polisher and the 'paps' were all wearing high reflective jackets with helmets next to their feet. Nevertheless, I was on a massive high and couldn't wait to get home and parade around the house like the proverbial awoken giant. Watch out E17, alert the courts trumpeter, your hero is approaching.

Oh no, O'Connor

The similarity with the Army and doing the Knowledge, for me, is relatively clear. Physically demanding, mentally challenging with an ever-changing problem to solve. I suppose that could be said for many a chaotic role in life but with the Knowledge, like military life, the aim is to mould you into the role. Now Mr O'Connor, although youthful in appearance, exuded some of the old school examiner character. Standing about six foot three, smartly turned out in nothing other than a well fitted grey, you could never imagine breaking that Stoney exterior during any appearance with him. Occasionally I heard the expression hard but fair when referring to Mr O'Connor. I was hoping the fair bit was more generous than the hard bit if ever I'd get to sit in the same room as him. The bike was running well. I had a bit of confidence behind me with my six points locked away and with four appearances left to score just twice I had a great chance of being on my 28-day appearances within six months or eight at the most. As with most work you do before an appearance, I'd try to mentally tick off the examiners I'd had before and who it left for me to have. The carriage office, like any workplace I suppose, would go through times when it didn't have that many examiners to share around and other times when they had loads. The PCO was going through one of those short-staffed periods when only a handful of examiners were appearing on the points sheets. This narrowed down the options giving all the Knowledge boys half a chance of guessing who you would have next time up. It was only guess work, but I'd go with the opinion of a fairground fortune teller if they had a reasonable view as to who I was up against next. I narrowed it down to Mrs Sadlier, as it had been a while since seeing her. Thomas maybe? because at that time it seemed just about everyone was having him and O'Connor as I'd never had him and he was always up the carriage office. For me, all three of these examiners had one characteristic about themselves that

I could try to steer my work towards. They all like big points. Cab driving areas like the West End, The City and Kensington. Nothing sneaky with these guys. When thinking about the hard but fair line it was a bang on description of all three of these masters of the map. The one thing you cannot do with big, well-known areas is get it wrong. It's like the trapeze artist has taken the wire away and given you a plank, if you fall off that you're never performing in the big top.

So, there I was, pushing Dutch around Euston and flying round the back of Kings cross station all the while eight hundred million pound was being spent on the soon coming grandeur of the new St Pancras station. In fact, with so much construction work going on, the biggest project in Europe at the time, you could hardly hear yourself think but that didn't take away the want to take a closer look at this vast space and wonder in awe of the level of planning it takes to accomplish an undertaking of this size. I flew past the soon to be 'grandest hotel' in London, the Midland. The building which lay only partially used for some thirty years gathering dust and cobwebs would soon become a living breathing giant once more. Named the Midland as this is the company that owned the railway track this giant beast of a building was now on its way to dominating the Kings Cross skyline. This old area had come a long way from the rumours that the great Iceni warrior Boudicca was buried beneath a thousand years' worth of earth under one of the platforms at the Cross. In my youth growing up in Kentish Town, Kings Cross was never a place to be visited either in the dark hours or alone. A place filled with people that shouldn't have been waiting for other people. A notorious drug invested, prostitution plagued hole. With the failing local authorities and disinterested private investment, The Cross was a haven for small cheap hotels catering for the less refined of clientele. Gone now are those days with the St Pancras Eurostar project underway and the rebuilding of the Midland and a new fancy loft apartment company cornering a part of this historic building for themselves. Soon the well-known chain stores and the coffee shops pandering to the new professional pound will arrive and finally transform the Cross into a more affluent and much regenerated centre north of the city. I know I've said this a few times but taking the Cross as an example there are sleeping giants all over this London of ours.

I remember the rain started as I reached the grand old entrance to Euston station. The war memorial outside remembers the 3,719 London and Western railway employees who gave their lives in the first world war. When you know this and look at the grandeur of the entrance, you wonder why the road planning authorities could not have designed a road plan which would have incorporated this and many other awe-inspiring entrances into still being the beginning of your journey and why we seem to have to use side entrances and silly makeshift ways into these emporiums of travel. I mean, redesign Euston Road, stick a little one way in or something and give us back an entrance that we can travel the world from. Who are these tightly browed planners who make everything so practical and forget that train travel could still hold thoughts of romance and windswept stories from far off lands. Alright, maybe the guy in the pin stripe suit doesn't feel much like Indiana Jones when he's clambering aboard the 18.05 to suburbia but you know what I mean. I was really working the big stations on my bike over those next few weeks.

Calling over about thirty or forty runs a day and the map was almost always on the kitchen table now. I'd even occasionally eat my dinner on top of the map. It always makes me laugh that I once sucked up a pea off the map which bounce off my dinner plate and right onto Penton Street, I'm surprised no one saw the news headline in the Evening Standard 'Giant pea rolls down towards Amwell Street'. My appearance was a nice late one, half past ten. Plenty of time to get my head together and get off down the Seven Sisters Road. I parked in the usual bike bays in Donegal Street and got straight into the Carriage Office as I needed to use the facilities. Typical, not a cubicle spare, mind you, these are nervous times just before facing your fate. I booked in and took the short walk to the waiting room. Nobody in there, another benefit of going in later, everyone's already been shot. I thought I'd take a sneaky look at the gigantic map on the wall when I heard 'Mr Syme?'. Covering the whole doorway was the smart, regimented, figure of Mr O'Connor. Straight into this, I couldn't believe it, no time to even feel nervous, I felt like I was on a roller coaster ride, before you even think you're up the top of the big hill you're on your way down. He asked me to take a seat and true to form he went straight for it and proved me right. Euston station to Charing Cross. Charing Cross to Lambeth North. Then they came. The two that would obviously make his mind up. Southfields station to Wandsworth Old town and Fulham Broadway station to Highbury corner. The second one there being the football run of Chelsea to Arsenal in disguise. Bang bang, both barrels. I imagined him dressed in full shooting tweed with a glass of port next to his Purdey shotgun. His prey now squeaking in front of him. As he looked me straight in the eye, I could hear the no score D galloping towards me. 'The first two were fantastic' he said, which sounded nice of him, but a child could have run those. 'But then you've had a lot of trouble southwest there don't you think?'. I couldn't argue but Southfields station to Wandsworth Old town was a cheeky little surprise in a quite forgotten part of town. Nevertheless, stations can't be dropped, or mis-run, and going down Merton Road instead of taking the right into Granville was a schoolboy error that told Mr O'Connor that me and Wimbledon were still to be acquainted. 'I think you're a nice guy and you'd make and good cab driver but, on this performance today, I can't score you' he offered my card back and said, 'you've got plenty of time, Mr Syme, have a little look at Wandsworth and take a few football runs out with you'. I didn't bother to explain that I'd already had two or three separate days of directional football runs over the past year. In fact, I'd been past so many of the clubs in London, I'd started to keep an eye on their progress throughout the leagues they were in and even the occasional root of support. I'd think of a certain face or two I'd seen on my travels would have been smiling with the latest victory. Mr O'Connor took a pride in his Knowledge. He'd done it himself, like everyone else up there. If you speak to any professional about their profession, they usually have a very high regard for their role and the path they led to get them there. Mr O'Connor was the same. He wasn't prepared to accept a lower standard of Knowledge as he wasn't given an easy path to get where he was today. Mr O'Connor, consistent.

Still three to go.

Two scores and a D. I still had three more appearances on this set to score twice, I knew I could do it. The bike was running well. Ok, she had a few more scratches than when I wheeled her out of old Johns that day, and the seat had a slight rip, but other than that, she was purring like a cat. The commute on the bike from my house in Walthamstow to my job at the bank in Lombard St, in the City. was going well enough. So really everything was in place to concentrate on my Knowledge and try to get through to my 28 day appearances in the next two.

I'd thought about joining a Knowledge school for some time now but never really got round to it. It makes me shake now, thinking every weekend spent out on my bike and most evenings spent calling over, or going through my tricky bits on the map I knew that it would be good for me to immerse myself with the same poor souls following the same lightless path, but I just kept delaying it. Not through fear of going but more that I was now going to really commit to all of this. To some people, they are their own best task master but when you tell the world what you're up to its then that you have some kind of hidden standard to keep. It's then that outside eyes may judge.

I was and never have been fearful of being new to any subject. You know what it's like when you meet someone who seems to know everything only because you are brand new to the subject only to find that when you have fully grasped it you look back at their command of the subject and realise, they didn't know that much after all. So, it wasn't the fear of walking into a school full of seasoned Knowledge boys and getting everything upside down. In fact, most Knowledge schools are extremely welcoming places full of likeminded people all aiming for the same outcome and through that togetherness discussion forums and, more importantly, learning takes place. Quintin Crisp said to never be afraid of failure and what courage he showed in his life. A tough call in those days of the Sweeney and the first Rocky films hitting the screens.

I thought I'd put off joining any school now as I thought I might be on a winner with my current work rate. A little routine at night after work. Half an hour of the blue book and half an hour of calling over, at random, any run on the appearance sheets. The problem you'll see here straight away is the 'at random' bit. When you're doing the Knowledge, such a sporadic subject, a study that is so unpredictable in its testing nothing can be left to chance. At random indicates that there could be gaps in things being left out in preference to others. This is the downfall of preparation. Fail to prepare and you prepare to fail. I didn't really understand at the time, but my plan wasn't the most watertight but although O'Connor gave me a little poke, I had scored two in a row before that so was still living on the memory of those successes. One of the problems about having such a long time in between appearances is that you are for ever whishing your time away. You can't wait for that time to elapse and get in the room and, hopefully, score. It really is wishing your life away. The time did fly by and before I knew it I was sitting in the waiting room waiting room nervously for my name to be called. I looked up from my nervous wait to discover a bright red-faced man with a very warming smile gazing right at me. If he calls my name I thought, how did he know to look at me, he was already scaring me with his fortune telling eyes. Sure enough, 'Mr Syme?' he said with his ever-broadening smile. 'Yes Sir' I said leaping up to attention. Down the corridor, I'm thinking to myself who the hell is this guy. We walk into a room I'd never been in before and he asks me to take a seat. Now my mind is racing. I'd never seen this guy before, was he even an examiner. Then beads of sweat started to form on my forehead. Maybe this guy is drafted in to deal with the Knowledge students that just can't be helped anymore. Maybe, as I take a seat, he'll sweep behind me and, holding me firmly around the head, whisper something like 'good night princess' as he turns my head to end, not only my never-ending grind but, also my wanting dreams.

I started to think all this was true and that he had an agent name like Q. He looked at my file, checked the picture clipped on the top was in fact me and then read a few of my past examiner's comments. 'Ok' he said exuding some calmness into my already boggling mind. 'What to do you know about Tavistock Square' smiling, he left me to answer the silence. 'Erm' I replied. 'There's a statue in the middle, do you know who that is'? he said. The light in my darkened brain came on. 'Ghandi sir' I said with eyes wider than a cow. 'Yep, that's him, do you know anything about him?' he said with a lovely smile. 'Erm' I said. 'Let me tell you a couple of things about Mr Ghandi' he said as I plumped up the pillows for a nice little story. It was times like this that these examiners would bestow upon you some great tit bits of information. It turns out that not only was Mahatma Ghandi, as the world knows him, the spiritual and political leader of India leading them through a time of independence but also a student studying to be a barrister in the Inns of court down the Temple in the City somewhere. I know he also stayed over there in bow at some point. A place called Kingsley Hall in E2. There is a blue plaque confirming Ghandi stayed there for a while, which is a lovely irony as the actor Ben Kingsley played Ghandi in the epic film. Q went on to tell me that Ghandi was against all forms of oppression and brought to the world Satyagraha, a form of mass peaceful protest. Put simply, if you mess about with us, we're simply not going to take it and we're going to sit down and do nothing. Ghandi also liked to go and sit on a hilltop somewhere once a month for a whole day and reflect. At this point Q's hidden message was starting to seep through. Reflect, take a step back, calm down and work out where it was all going wrong. Q was turning out to be the spiritual light sent to guide me through. After the lesson in the Indian political scene of the 1930's I came back down from spiritual enlightenment and was asked by Q to run Russell Square to Kings Cross station. Watch it Q, I know your trying to get me to go around Tavistock Square I don't want any charity here. Well, in fact I do, but a little bit of self-merit as well. The appearance flew by. I'd done well. Knowledge school would be put on the back burner at this rate, and I'd sail this ship alone. Q finished with some nice words about it all being a process you must go through to reach the other side and we'll all get to wherever we're all going in the end. This guy had a candle burning gently in his heart. I felt like I'd been massaged back into the booking out hall. I knew I'd scored but in a way this euphoria was overshadowed by Q's calmness and polite wisdom. I found out from a couple of conversations with the points collectors outside that Q was a nice man called Mr Field. I'd heard good reports of Mr Field before but because I'd never remembered any description of him, didn't know what I was up against but, through his power of calmness and teachings of Ghandi, I'd never forget him. When I came back down to reality, I'd accumulated nine points. I could taste 28's now. I was feeling powerful with this subject now. I was being told through having nine points that I was on my way. Gone would be my corporate life and the door of freewheeling survival was fast approaching.

Wobble wobble

Seven Sisters Road. Named after seven trees that stood here many moons ago, well the 1800's anyway. I heard they were all named after the children of an old dignitary of Scotland. I have been told by locals, that the junction of Seven Sisters and Tottenham high road used to be called Wards Corner after a great big department store that stood there once. The famous singer Shirley Bassey once lived here long before gaining fame and fortune. I suppose after she'd earned her first million, she'd had enough of the Victoria Line and could never get a parking space in Wickes builders' merchants across the road that she decided to move. For a good few year now, early in the morning, labourers, builders hands and general work seekers have hung about on the corner of Wickes waiting for small builders vans to turn up to offer a day's work. On some mornings, you could have up to forty men standing around waiting to be picked for the day by passing builders. I remember growing up, that was quite the norm for local hands to assemble on the corners of Kilburn High Road, to wait the same chance meeting. With the gathering crowd comes the general chat with others in the same position and enough cigarettes are being smoked that when all is done, and the men leave these corners, it looks like a man and a horse have been cremated there.

Travelling towards this crowd one bright morning, doing about 26 miles per hour, see, Dutch could get going when she wanted, was obviously not a good time for Dutch to strike a discarded nail in the road and send me on a comical looking wobble straight towards three surprised looking Eastern Europeans. I don't know what 'cor blimey' is in Polish but I'm sure that was one of the phrases used, if not a little stronger. With my full-face helmet shielding only the height of my eyebrows, I headed towards the builders. My eyes were as wide as theirs as I had what felt like a small circus clown pulling my back wheel from left to right. Before I crashed into the three guys standing there smoking, I just remember thinking, surely, I can't hit all three of you. As I looked up, all I could see where two of the builders standing over me, obviously escaping the impact of little old Dutch, still smoking their cigarettes, which I thought was impressive. There were three of them. Just before raising my head from the pavement, I looked to my right, and there, rubbing his leg, inside a perfectly torn pair of Wrangler jeans, was the third labourer moaning something in Polish. 'Ouch me pe, ajuda' he kept repeating. Turns out he's Portuguese, and roughly translated he was crying, ouch my leg, which was understandable. I said sorry maybe twenty times before wheeling Dutch up Seven Sisters in the direction of Walthamstow. In the distance I could still here the Portuguese guys, 'Cissy' I heard one of them say, which it seems means Cissy in Portuguese. Poor fella. He's just standing on a street corner trying to get some work when, suddenly, he's confronted by an old M reg Honda that could have at least had a wash in the past couple of years. They weren't too impressed, but didn't take it any further, which was an old school move, so respect to them.

As I pushed Dutch home, yep, Seven Sisters to the top of Forest Road must be two miles, I realised that wearing full waterproof outfit and full-face helmet on a nice bright day is sometimes not the best of ideas. By the time I'd reached home, lord knows how long it took, I must have lost a stone in body weight. I'm thinking of bringing out my own exercise video advising how to get down to your ideal body weight using only a Honda C-90 and twenty-six layers of clothing. The whole days' work put on hold. I'd taken a day off work, planned it all out. I was starting with Islington and all those squares and then I'd move onto windswept Highgate and maybe pop in and see the tomb of Karl Marx in the cemetery but alas, it'll have to wait until Dutch gets a patch and a little air in the boots.

Eventually, the puncture was sorted out by a local bike mechanic shop that used to be a Butchers on Forest Road E17. Strange thing is, by the look of some of the Hells Angels that visited the place, you didn't really know that they hadn't stopped cutting up meat in there as some of them looked like they were partial to the odd blood bath of some sort or another.

I got all the work done throughout the coming few weeks and being so engrossed in my progress, arrived at my appearance day. This was a big appearance. If I score today, I'd be on twenty eights. I could virtually say I'm nearly finished with just twenty ones and the suburbs to take on. The booking in queue was massive. I'd never seen the room so busy. Every face, in every office, was moving around. Examiners were coming into the booking hall to collect the files of their next victims. The Knowledge boys' heads were turning left, right and centre to catch glimpses of who was going where. Not only was I up for my drop and trying to contend with my own big day, but the place had turned into a City trading room. My heart was racing. I could see Knowledge boys taking deep breaths around the water machine. One bloke was even doing leg and arm stretches, this was serious. 'Smith' cried out Thomas. 'Johnson' bellowed Wilkins. Looks like the examiners were dealing with their own excitement by cracking through the appearances and names one a minute. I'd have no time to think in this chaos. If my examiner comes out just as excited as everyone around them then I'd have to think on my feet with this one.

Every seat, and I mean every seat, in the waiting room was filled. There we were being called one a minute and you could see previously called knowledge boys trudging down the corridor to the booking hall. It was all too busy to even consider how they got on, today was every man for himself. Another couple of names later and Courtney swung his head round, 'Mr Syme, up up up' he shouted. He'd obviously been taken in by the chaos but who could blame him, it was like the Alamo here. Up I got, we flew towards his office,

I'd forgotten how important this one was for me. Down we sat, he wasted no time. Merton Road to Chelsea Harbour. Whoa there, SW19 off the bat, this was exciting but big stuff for me. Done that, he raised his eyebrow but nothing serious. Lots Road to the Michelin building in Fulham Road, it was elementary. Brompton Oratory to the Parrot club inside the Basil Street hotel, thought he'd get me on that one, but I got the point and away I went. He stopped it. Right there and then, Courtney stopped the appearance and gave me back my card. Three runs and out the room. The chaos outside must have contributed to such a quick appearance. I couldn't believe it, one of the biggest days of my Knowledge to date and I didn't even realise it was happening. Three runs, less than the usual four or five and I'd got my drop to 28's. I shook his hand, that's how pleased I was. I'd touched an examiner. You don't touch these people. You don't call them by their first names, and you definitely don't hug them, but he nearly got one that day. I could feel a skip developing as I went towards the booking hall. How strange it felt when the booking clerk looked up and said well-done see you back here on the 4th. It was very strange hearing that the date of which he'd said was so close, in fact it was 28 days closer than my 56-day appearance. I went from 56-day appearances to 28 days appearances and couldn't have been happier.

Sitting down that night with a bottle of beer, and a delivered Pizza from the infamous Walthamstow Pizza GO GO, I couldn't wait to skip into work and take a good look around the office in the way that someone who's going on holiday would, prior to departure. Only a few more months and I'd be out of here.

Now you're with the big boys.

I knew, just knew, that at this level there would be no prisoners taken. At 28 days you are, or should be, at the height of your London Knowledge. At 21's they know you've done the work so the examiners will just be looking for you to hone those skills and maybe have a general knowledge of the tricks of the trade and be a bit more 'savvy on the lingo'. At 28's though, you were expected to be red hot. There would be no second chances. The questions would be harder with a lot more one-way puzzles and restrictions to deal with. These appearances would take in all those little problems that make London Taxi drivers the best in the world. Where once I would merrily pop out on my bike and tick off all those places I'd seen on the appearance sheets and say I knew them, now I would really have to know them. I said to my great friend Jeff, who had been doing the knowledge for some time now, that if I don't call the run, who will? He laughed, but we both saw a truth in the saying. When you're sitting in front of an examiner, it's only you that will tell that examiner how to get from A to B. He's not there to help you. It's the same as when a tourist comes to London and jumps in a cab and says a name of an obscure hotel, and it's their first time to this great city. They don't know a thing about the place so it's all up to you to get them to that unheard of hotel in one piece.

Jeff had been on more levels than the Trump tower. His method of let the knowledge come to you had its flaws. Through all of his chequered path, he'd never lost his cool. Jeff didn't believe in Knowledge schools. I thought one day I'd have to pop along to see what all the fuss was about. Me and Jeff spent a lot of time together in the early stages of the Knowledge, but like all things in life, we'd occasionally follow different paths to the same ending.

The camaraderie we shared calling over the bluebook, and laughs we had at each other's expense were great times, but we both knew that being so close and friendly was no way to knuckle down and get this stuff done. I would accuse Jeff of peeking at the sheet before a call over session and he'd always say I was mis-pronouncing road names and couldn't follow my lines on the map as he'd never heard of half the roads I was calling. It was like watching a comedy sketch.

Now that 28's was here, I felt professional. I would have to confront all my demons. I would have to look at those back roads in Clapham and promised not to leave a stone un-turned in Shoreditch and the City just in case Mr Wilkins threw down the gauntlet one day. Football runs were being knocked out every weekend in between trying to replenish the fragments of a social life either at home or at work. The workload started to beckon full time study. That's one of the things I heard a cab driver say to me once, that the Knowledge and cab driving was for those who'd missed the boat. He was trying to say that there are a lot of cab drivers out there that, although were good enough and intelligent enough for that degree or prosperous career, had other things in the way or just didn't use the effort at the right time. Of course, there are some drivers out there who have got all the qualifications to follow an academic career but through the lure of such a flexible life chose the Knowledge and this strange self-employment. You see so many drivers diversify and do other things once they have the badge and that was another attraction for me. Just think, I thought, I could go into acting and never worry about the high rate of unemployment as I'd have the badge.

I could write and maybe look for a little niche market business somewhere. The possibilities, if not endless, were varied. When you think, being of retirement age and being able to still go out, in the cab, and get more than your pension in one day must be a big draw to keep the badge in old age.

It was no secret that I was in line for a right tough appearance on my first 28. The examiner, whoever I get, would know to give me a good kick up the backside and pull me to shreds so that I would go away and think this level wasn't for muppets. The Knowledge was now running my life. Anywhere I was, I'd be reading the address of anything to see if it was in London and check if I knew it. There were times when I would read the address off a junk mail flyer and, if it came from London somewhere, would try to call it to and from the Carriage office. My mind was full of the Knowledge. I would watch any TV programme that was filmed or related to London in anyway, The Bill, Eastenders and even old re-runs of Minder and The Sweeney, just so as I could hear or see anything relating to the subject. Crazy I know, but I have seen Knowledge boys with Lap top computers, making camcorder recordings of their travels and even Jeff's Knowledge boy neighbour, who used to take a photo of every point he'd seen. Imagine four thousand photos in your house of Police Stations, Hospitals, public buildings, and the odd alleyway. Everything was about London in the end. I would think of a friend who lived in one part of London, and call every road to another friend's house regardless of if they knew each other or that I hadn't even seen either of them for years. Work, real paying work I mean, was doing its best to try and get in the way but I was managing to keep the corporate beast at bay for the time being.

Oh no, not again.

I sat in front of Mr O'Connor for my first 28 knowing the outcome before taking the seat. I don't think I could ever score against him anyway let alone having him sent in like the assassin for this one. The rumour at the time was that he, and Courtney, had just had enough of Knowledge boys not knowing their stuff. The blow was hard, but inevitable. I took it like a man, and before the seat was even warm, he'd given me back my card. He looked disgusted with me. Although I knew this would be the most likely outcome after this appearance, I didn't think I'd feel this bad, but I'd immersed myself so much over the past 28 days that you always secretly hope for a brighter ending, I think that's hope in general, isn't it? He didn't say one word. I had to assume I was finished and opened the door out of his office like I'd been told there was no second chances for the likes of me. Everything around me was a blur as I booked out. The points collectors wanted my attention, but I just walked past. It's on days like this that the more experienced points collectors know to leave you alone. I walked along Penton Street turned left into Donegal Street to the waiting Dutch and slowly started to change into my bike gear.

I only had a half morning off work for this one. Knowing that it would probably end in disappointment, the plan was to take the morning off work, then if it all went wrong, I could the just stick my head down and get on with forgetting about the day. I could forget about not scoring and it would look like I was a productive employee at the bank. It would look like I was serious about doing well in the office and maybe progressing to higher levels. It reminds me of the scene in the Eddie Murphy film, Coming To America, where, as the King of a small Fijian Island, Eddie Murphy gets himself a job in a burger bar to interact with 'normal' people and, while talking with one of the employees there, is told by this guy making burgers 'this time next year, I'll be on Lettuce and that's where the real bucks come in'. We all have our own goals, whatever the size. Little did they know that the work would be just a shield and a temporary wall that held up an otherwise decaying and crumbling study regime.

Oh, to call her Nicola

Always a feeling of accomplishment, getting someone, who has such a Stoney exterior, to like you. This would only be a hope and dream concerning my efforts with Ms Danvers. Bruce Lee like in her appearance. Small, petite like, but every inch iron. This lady could look into the soul of the most reverent of people and frighten the living begeebees out of them. A face that was permanently concentrating, with an exterior that only her closest lifelong friends could break. Like all examiners, always very well presented with an air of superiority. I never saw this lady in anything but a well-fitting grey business suit. I longed for the day, while waiting to be called, to smell the waft of summery perfume and the glimpse of a strawberry covered knee-high dress befitting the Wimbledon tennis month of flaming June. She would walk in and, with the whole room becoming cloudy, gently whisper…. 'Mr Syme'? I'd drift out of my seat, and, before I knew it, gazing deep into those dark eyes while she delivered my appearance with the ease and finesse of a Swiss finishing school graduate. WHOA, WHOA, hold on a dam minute here. This is Danvers. The only finishing school that would have complimented her standards would have been the military academy at Sandringham where one learns all manner of commands. She could throw a martial arts star at your neck from two hundred feet away and, as it imbedded itself into your jugular vein, turn and finish her water melon breakfast. Maybe the grey suit wasn't grey, it was gun metal. I mean, real gun metal, not the fashionistas colour gun metal grey. More a suit of armour. Ready for any eventuality.

I wondered of the rumour that if you tried hard, and kept an eye on her every move, that towards the top of her shoulder, you could see the S.A.S crest and motto, Who Dares Wins tattooed. My eyes could not get any bigger when hearing that one but, as I quickly found out, the last thing that is ever true is Knowledge boy rumours.

I've heard some cracking rumours in these circles. To name but a few, the guy who done his Knowledge driving around with a camcorder strapped to handlebars. The easy ride given to ex-servicemen, and how the odd three points are slung their way. The completely illegal buying of green badges for thousands of pounds. Yeah, try buying a badge, throwing it around your neck and then getting a plated cab and then going out to work. On every level, this obviously wouldn't work. They know your shoe size before you get out in these cabs. Just a few rumours that get in the way of the real work of doing the Knowledge.

At the time I laughed at the S.A.S Danvers rumour. I even flicked through a couple of the Andy McNab novels just to see whether I could pick up any tips for self-defence just in case one day I fell foul of the Danvers scowl. Size has never been a good enough measure for heart and conviction. I knew that if Miss Danvers had me in a half nelson, she wouldn't blink an eye in twisting my neck for the ultimate conclusion. I had to prepare. I'd got my work in order, and the closer it got to judgement day I could feel a showdown with Danvers was due. I'd never caught her eye in the waiting room or out in the booking hall. I'd rarely been in the waiting room when she had come in to drag a poor unfortunate out so there was really no history to go on.

As usual, I reflected on all the examiners I'd had, and it looked a fair chance I should be having Danvers sooner or later. It's a funny thing, but the chances of getting this right are about 25-1, but, after being around the appearance track a few times, you really do get a feel for how it works in a strange chaotic way. The Knowledge was always there, lingering about in the background like a forgotten friend, but expecting my first daughter Molly put everything into perspective. Even the Knowledge, and the enormity of the mountain I was climbing, was put into a manageable way expecting a little baby. That's the thing with the Knowledge, you're living a life through it all as well. At the time all this was happening, I thought I was still on my game. You can't do all this though and for it not to influence your study, it's just life.

By the time I'd got up for my second appearance of 28's I was already losing track of what had come out on the appearance sheets and wasn't really calling over my blue book so much. As I was clouded in impending family life, and all the challenges and dreams that brings with it, I lost touch with furthering my Knowledge to the level needed. Donegal Street, change at the bike, book in and a quick sip of water from the machine.

Pop into the toilet, and I'd followed my pre appearance routine to the letter, shame I'd didn't follow my work routine before I got up there. I'd had a good reason, but you're never asked for a reason.

As predicted, the names were being called out from the waiting room by every other examiner than Danvers. I was quietly patting myself on the back when it happened. My eyes were fixed to the floor when out of the corner of my eye I saw gun metal grey. Before I had chance to look up, I heard 'Mr Syme'. I sprang up and, in a pure automated fashion, I done something that I'd regret for the rest of my days. 'Yes Sir' I replied. Clunk! I'd called Ms Danvers sir. One Knowledge boy almost fainted, while another made the sign of the cross on his chest. I stood flabbergasted at my mistake. 'Do I look like a Sir' she bellowed at me, in the middle of the waiting room. I mumbled and apologised and apologised again. All I wanted to do was fall to my knees and scream 'No no no' and plea for another chance before the sword would be inserted into my chest. She left the room expecting me to follow, which I did like a dutiful puppy. I could feel a twitch on my eye developing, and I felt like I needed food to increase my blood/sugar levels. She sat down and told me to close the door and, before I could sit down, mumbled the word 'sir' under her breath. As I sunk into the chair, I'd forgotten everything I'd seen in Andy McNab's novels. I was hers for the taking. I fought I was going to die by a slightly raised shoe heel in my left eye. Instead, in a macabre tone, she went straight into asking for Chariots Spa in Shoreditch to Highgate West Hill. A nice long one to start with. Then, still tight lipped, she asked for the Carriage Office to Kings Cross….and return. I was just about keeping up but not feeling too well with it. If there was one thing this appearance was doing it was working my mouth as there were so many roads to call. Arsenal Football club to Charlton football club, these were massive runs. Lastly, two points I'd dropped and then I went on to drop all the other points she asked me at both ends of the run she wanted. It was like a stale mate. I couldn't start or finish this last one. Her eyes fixed on me like a bird of prey. Like a cat ready to pounce. My lines needed a lot of work. I needed to look at more points and, most of all, I need to find out the difference between sir and ma'am. Her arm was extremely straight when she handed back my card. Stern to the very end.

So, two appearances on 28's, and two D's. Five more to score three times, there was still a chance. I could be on 21's in about four months given a couple of close shaves thrown in. I had to start to separate life from study. The study needed to take higher ground to get through this, then life could finally be enjoyed. Getting back after any appearance always had its opposites. There was the hollow feeling of failure but also the warm secure feeling of home. I drove Dutch through the kitchen and out the back door into the garden. I promised to clean up the tyre tracks in the hallway as I waited for the fumes to clear. A nice bowl of soup and a reflection of the day's events. Onwards and upwards.

Using my loaf

The study of the Knowledge is one of those missions in life that you take up for many a different reason. Some make the decision to have a more flexible way of working. Some make the decision to work around an already growing family, others make the decision in the search for, as some people say, the golden cow, money. I have always thought that if you enter any profession with the only goal being money you are always going to lay yourself open to a lack of certain standard. Hopefully I am right in my reason to study the Knowledge which was to have a flexible working life to fit around the plan of a family later in life. One of the other major factors to get on this merry path was my overriding interest in London and all that's within. Concentrate on the quality and the money will soon follow. I think this attitude should be employed in most areas of life. The craftsman who does a job well for the sake of doing it well., not lead by prize but passion. Anyway, I'd got used to commuting from Highams Park on the East London/Essex boarder. Either on my bike or, on the train straight into Liverpool Street, twenty minutes. Generally, life was getting busier, and I was cramming in work wherever I could, but I needed to get on with my Knowledge, I needed time, I needed reflection, I needed……Ghandi.

I hadn't seen South London in a while. Looking around the somewhat grimy, and in need of serious funding, Elephant and Castle, you can see the London thing of neighbouring stark contrast. One minute you're dodging bullets around the tip of Newington Butts only to fall into some of those picturesque Georgian squares a stone's throw away.

I like Kennington, always have. The squares speak for themselves. Walcott, Cleaver, all leafy and hidden from the busy main streets. Well-kept by the residents too. Newington Butts, joining the Elephant to Kennington Park Road, so named because there was an Archery site around the area that would train archers from all over the land. A butt, I've heard, was a term for the target used. Ian Dury used Newington Butts as rhyming slang for guts in his song Blackmail Man, so, notoriety all round.

Kennington Park road leading to Clapham Road is so straight it's no surprise that it forms part of an old roman road. You've got to give it to the romans on many different levels and particularly roads, they did build 'em straight. Doing the Knowledge in Roman times would have been a doddle. London Bridge station to Chichester please? sure Sir, get on Newington Butts, point south westerly and don't turn the chariots wheels for about eighty miles. Edward the third gave the manor of Kennington to his son, also called Edward. They love keeping a name them royals. He was known as, possibly the best name to be known as, The Black Prince. What a wonderful title. It conjures up thoughts of capes and silhouettes jumping roof tops in the dead of night but, unfortunately, is now only represented by the road of the same name leading from Albert Embankment to Kennington Park Rd. I read once that it was the Manor of Edward the third, although I was told by a van driver, in no uncertain terms, that this was his manor, and I should leave immediately or something to that effect.

The social reform group of Chartists met a few times on Kennington Common, a piece of land now covered by St Marks church yard and Kennington Park itself. History records that on this very common the occasional execution would take place. I read somewhere that nine leaders of the Jacobite revolution were executed there in about 1746. In those days, Kennington common would have been almost countryside so to take the convicted down that way to end their days hanging from a rope would have been out of sight for the busier part of town to see. Although executions throughout London's history have normally been a big crowd puller, this sight was for endings that the authorities thought wouldn't be a big-ticket seller. I'm sure if any self-respecting promoter had been around in those days, they could have drummed up a bit more interest, and had a small German market going on down there as well.

Michael Faraday, the great Chemist and Physicist was born in Newington Butts and apart from his work in the investigative fields of electric conductors he invented a very early version of the Bunsen Burner. As every naughty schoolboy knows, the Bunsen Burner was a great way of spending a boring Science lesson burning your friends' fingers or seeing who could hold their finger over that flame the longest, so a big thank you to Mr faraday for those years spent mystified by the blue flame.

There's a lot to this place but what gets me is the leafy squares and the serenity that is found off the beaten track. Some of the locals have told me they have quite a few foxes drifting in and out of Kennington although, as one local told me, I don't think they get down the Elephant that often as it's a bit rough down that end of town.

Not what you think

The Italian author Dante wrote a book called the Divine Comedy (or inferno if you want to get technical) in which he describes seven different layers of hell. Each level befitting the crime and the worse the crime the lower you go.

On the bottom level is the body of Judas Iscariot encased in Ice with his eyes wide open to be made aware of the enormity of his crime for eternity in punishment for pointing out (the kiss) Jesus Christ for crucifixion. In the book, Dante describes different symbols for different sins and human tragedy. The symbol of treachery is the face of an innocent, kind looking man, but with the tale of the devil.

My third appearance on 28's. I hadn't even felt like I had a chance on the other two. I'd come up against two big guns in O'Connor and Danvers. I felt that because I'd faced two of the toughest examiners there were at the time, I may stand a chance with my next one. I stepped up my blue book calling over and I was still getting out on my bike enough to know everything was still in its place for me to ride down to the Carriage Office and try to extract three points out of this next appearance. I got down to Donegal Street nice and early and would you believe there were no spaces for me to put Dutch in. If I'd learnt anything about parking around Islington, it was 'take no chances. I thought I might be able to squeeze Dutch on the end of the solo motorbike bay but if I leave one wheel hanging over, I've had it. The traffic warden would be there before I could get my trousers off and another sixty quid ticket would be in my possession.

I took a little ride around and found another bay a few roads away. This bay was right outside someone's kitchen window, so I think they were a little shocked when I started getting my waterproofs off outside their house and slowly re-dressing. I think the little old lady watching me from her sink was thinking, is it a bird? is it a plane? no, it's another star gazing Knowledge boy hoping for some kind of life to come out of the Public Carriage Office.

Fully dressed and trying to hide another pre ironed but now totally creased shirt, I walked off to the sound of the Rocky theme tune Eye of the Tiger rolling around in my head. I even greeted the points collectors on the door as I approached, something I'd never done before due to being lost in nerves and thought. I looked like I was saying 'Morning guys, I'll be out shortly with three points and a list of my appearance runs, won't be long'.

Having Booked in, I was just about to leave the booking hall when I heard someone at one of the other windows say, 'Hello there, I'd like the forms to do the Knowledge please'. I nearly turned round and threw myself at his ankles pleading with him not to get on this rocky road. Save your own life, be nice to your partner and enjoy what you have, no no no. I just opened the door and left shaking my head.

I walked into the waiting room and who was there? Jeff. I couldn't believe it. All this time spent doing the Knowledge and our paths had never crossed.

In fact, I'd never bumped into anyone I'd ever seen or known in the waiting room but now opposite me was my mate, Jeff. 'Whey hey, alright?' I said, full of the joys of spring. He just stared straight ahead. He was in a trance like state of nerves. I suppose I was trying to get rid of mine by talking and wanting to unload a mountain of thoughts. Jeff had decided to take the

Shaolin Monk route and meditate it out. He was like a different person. I'd grown up with this guy all my life but now I could have struck a match under his nose, and he wouldn't have flinched. That's how it can get to you. To Jeff's relief, I was called first. I suppose me trying to get through to him had taken my mind off waiting and there I am with my name being called. Up I got not even realising who had called my name when I turned the corner, I saw I was following Mr Field. A nice gentle man with a brilliant red face. If he wasn't so nice you would say this man liked a drop or two of malt whiskey and was a bit sharp round a card table. I've since learned that he is very skilful in motor mechanics and could tell you one end of an engine to another from fifty paces. The suit was a good quality pin stripped number with, would you believe, a red silk handkerchief in the triangular fashion poking out from the top pocket, class. He asks me to take a seat. He asks me how I was. I felt I was relaxing. Then he asks me the digress Bar in Beak Street off Regent Street to the Dominion Theatre stage door in Bainbridge Street, relax over. I couldn't believe this kind looking man was delivering such tough questions with such a warm smile. He then said from that same stage door to the British Massage school in Newman Passage off Newman Street. Even when I found out where that was, I didn't want to go down there as it was so small and creepy, I thought I'd just rely on where it was rather than seeing it. I was trying to go surfing on an Ironing board.

Luck had left as soon as I'd sat down and my third D in a row, on 28's, was served by this quiet, kind looking man. Never had bad news been given so kindly. I booked out in total desperation. I had four appearances left to score three times. I was looking for seventy five percent when I hadn't even mustered one yet. What chance was I facing. I didn't want to think about being red lined on 28's. To go back to 56's day appearances from here would be embarrassing. It would mean that after nearly three years work, I would be virtually back to the beginning. I had to liven this whole thing up. New approaches, new sacrifices had to be made. I would have to look at my job at the bank, the time it was taking up, and I would definitely have to look at involving myself with a Knowledge school, it had to help.

I walked down the stairs dreading seeing the points collectors that I'd been so confident in seeing forty minutes earlier. I reached the door, and as I went out into Penton Street, there, with all the colour back in his face, was Jeff. The nerves had gone from his face. He looked relieved. It looked like he scored but he then went on to explain he also got a D, but he was just pleased it was over until next time. We decided to drown our sorrows in the Star café opposite and treated ourselves to a big breakfast. We sat in there with other Knowledge boys on the other tables. Burly men wearing ill-fitting suits. As we tucked into the Star cafes best sausages, the door came open and in walked the lively personality that was P.C.O examiner, Mr Courtney. Although we were all equal out in Public, away from the system of the Public Carriage Office, all the tables nodded to him and called him Sir. I was going to offer him my last sausage and maybe wash it down with my milky coffee in line for favourable result next time. On reflection, if bribery was a route, something more enticing than a half-burnt banger and mug of slurp would have to be offered. Chatting and going over each other's appearances was a nice finish to an otherwise disastrous day and, although trying to help each other out, as we looked onto a blustery Penton Street and the bland facade of the Carriage Office, we knew that we'd have to change. You can help each other as much as you want but if it's not in your head when you reach that seat in the appearance room well, who's going to call the run?

I'd taken to typing out all my roads, runs and points that I was a bit sketchy on and cutting them up into tiny little pieces of paper to compile a pocket-sized book of trouble spots so I could carry them about wherever I went. This little book was especially handy on my occasional train journeys to work. I could sit there and run over all the rubbish without having to get out heap loads of paperwork, looking like some sort of Scientist working on a new discovery. I also came to the idea that, like I've said before, if I wasn't going to call it then no one else was going to do it for me in that dreaded room. I called over any run I could get my hands on. Some of the routes and lines that were showing up on that map were completely bizarre but at least I was going all over London in my head and there's no better place to get it all wrong than away from the examiners. In the end, I wanted to get things wrong so I could start getting them right, if you get my drift. All the sweat and tears should happen out of sight of the PCO. When you go up there and sit in the waiting room with the rest of them, that's showtime. That's the time when you're dressed to kill and it's the chance for all the hard work to speak for itself. I was becoming a Knowledge zombie. Most of the time my attention span was only limited to the Knowledge. Although with little Molly here now, I did have glimmers of a real life, but I think anyone would agree that it's coming to something when the birth of your first baby just about beats a subject you're studying to the popularity stakes. Then again, just how important is the Knowledge to Knowledge students. It engulfs your life, it puts things on hold and, after a long enough time, changes the character of the person pursuing the elusive green badge. It is a life changer. For good or bad, it doesn't fail to have an everlasting effect on those who continue. Talking of life changing moments, we'd been getting into our stride with the birth of little Molly when news came through the maternal grapevine of a baby boy, Harry. Wonderful. Look out for the film, babies, and badges. Anyway, that was the tiny duo sorted, now for an accomplishment of another kind.

Stranger things have happened.

I woke up on the morning of the appearance thinking only of one thing. If I don't score, that's three and a bit years down the swanny. Three years of blood, sweat and tears. Three years of hope and disappointment. Three years of sitting on Dutch wishing I was sitting in a cab, sorry Dutch! Some of the streets I'd been down so often that I now felt at home in them. I'd become a regular in a barber shop in Green Lanes when never living, working, or socialising in the area. I was on waving terms with newsagents in Marylebone and nodding terms with sandwich shops in Paddington. I knew where the toilets were in several different pubs when never even had a drink in the places. Recognising the barman or that they had a new fruit machine. I'd put layers on this life of mine and now I was facing an appearance which would say that I'd wasted that time. Looking back at all those places and those people, becoming part of so many different areas, how you could possibly say any of that was wasted. A beautiful experience of life.

I got dressed slowly. I concentrated on my breathing. I made sure I felt clean and presentable. I'd booked that whole day off work for this one. This appearance wasn't the kind I could just shrug off if I failed to score. This one would hurt. Even if I did score, I knew I was still up against it but, if I did, it would say to me that the examiners might have taken me to the line like this to say more effort was needed and a jolly good fright was in order.

I took the train. There was no way I could ride little Dutch home if it went badly. I was the only person in the waiting room. The silence was deafening. I heard the occasional laugh from outside the waiting room and thought how far away from that free feeling I was right now. I tried to console myself by thinking that there were people in the world who weren't doing the Knowledge. Any moment, I could leave this life of purgatory and resume a normal existence busy planning fun things like holidays and nights out. This is the route of failure I thought. If we never put ourselves up for the challenge, how would anything worth completing be achieved.

I continued with the heroic thoughts as these were starting to calm me. I thought of the SAS trooper Chris Ryan who, when behind enemy lines ran the longest escape by any soldier and had to run over two hundred miles to safety. I reflected on the only other guy to match such a feat, Jack Stilleto, another SAS trooper, who ran through the Sahara Desert back in 1942. There I was thinking of heroes, and overcoming adversity, and all I wanted was three points on my scorecard. Then, stood in the doorway, like Clubber Lang waiting for Rocky to enter the ring, was the master of the east. The Shoreditch specialist. The prince of darkness himself, Mr Wilkins. His runs were never long, just extremely fiddly. He had routes up his sleeve where he only wanted you to go across the road but, due to several road restrictions, you would have to call out six or seven roads and most of them small and tricky to remember. Rumour was that Mr Wilkins, apart from already having the Cab driving green badge of London, was studying for the other extremely hard badge to acquire, the tourist guides blue badge. This gave Mr Wilkins a very knowledgeable demeanour. Every time I saw Mr Wilkins, he would be wearing a St Georges cross lapel pin on his jacket. The jacket pin, coupled with his handlebar like moustache and deep throated actor like voice, gave Mr Wilkins the air of the old English land-owning gentry. I'm sure, like most Knowledge students, Mr

Wilkins came from a humble background, although you could never tell, as to all and sundry he gave the impression you were dealing with someone of complete authority in whichever subject would be discussed.

He called my name, and I could feel my legs weaken as I left the seat. I followed Mr Wilkins into his office and shut the door very gently as if not to disturb any karma in the room. He asked me to 'grab' a seat which I thought was quite informal for him to use such a term. I thought if he was going to start using friendly lingo then I might stand a chance of already being in his good books.

After gazing at my file for about two or three minutes, which seemed like an eternity, he looked up and said....'do you like a massage Mr Syme?'. I couldn't believe my ears. In the three years I'd been doing the Knowledge, and listening to Knowledge boy rumours, you learn that nothing was ever asked without a reason. I looked down at the floor thinking of any connection with massages in London, and then it came to me, the London massage school in Newman Passage off Newman Street. I'd already been asked that by Mr Field. 'You know, do you like someone rubbing your shoulders' he interrupted my thought. I jolted back into the room and said, 'I don't mind sir'. With my answer still floating in the air, he threw out Chariots spa and massage in Fairchild Street. A tricky little side alley in Shoreditch. To the Stanstead express entrance of Liverpool Street station. It can only be half a mile. Already I was wobbling about. Before I had chance to finish the run, he asked for Browns table dancing bar, officially in Hackney Road, to Sid's tea hut in Cavell Street, Arnold circus. All East, and to me, all tricky.

The thing with Mr Wilkins' East runs was they always had just one key road or puzzle to sort out. If you didn't know that road, or the little trick to the run, you had no chance. He asked questions where he just wanted to hear that one road get called and the rest he didn't bother with. He didn't hear what he wanted to hear. The room fell silent. It was obvious that I hadn't scored but with the weight of three and a bit years of service given to the knowledge I also couldn't see that he could put me all the way back to the start.

After looking again at my file, he wrote something on my card and as he lifted his arm to give me it back, he said 'ok Mr Syme, we'll see you back hear in..... he delayed as if checking he had it right....'56 days.

Bang, I don't think I even said goodbye out of shock. I don't think I even looked at him as I took my card back. I'm sure I heard him say something like you'll be OK, but I wasn't even sure he said that. Everything I'd done, everyone I'd seen and spoke to about this subject in the last three years had come crashing down. This was no minor delay. This was a setback of such an extent, I would have to think about continuing. I would have to judge whether it was right or not for me to carry on this grey path.

I must have booked out and walked straight past the points collectors. I must have boarded the train back home but all of this, even to this day, is a complete blur. I knew the feeling of numbness and depression would be with me for a long time. I knew that it wouldn't just go away with a good night out and that I would wake occasionally in the dark with an empty feeling of despair.

I didn't mean to take a break from any Knowledge work for the next week or two, but it just didn't seem like something that came to mind. Apart from the fact that through complete rejection I now had 56 days in between each appearance and this, although I didn't want it, had given me more time. Something, I suppose, the carriage office thought I needed. During this period of 'anti' Knowledge, I fell back into my life. Socialised with family and friends in the hope of helping me to forget. I was flicking through T.V channels and found myself watching a programme about the foreign legion. OK, it was a bit drastic, but I needed something to shake the cobwebs of life off. I needed something to put a little bit of colour back into it all. Something I could have some fun with.

Monopoly, A geographical nightmare

I like a jog. I suppose it started as a weight losing thing but then developed into a full-scale pastime. My usual jogging plan is to run half an hour in one direction and then turn around and run back. Nothing complicated, no stopwatches or performance enhancing liquids just a pair of shorts with two chewing gum white legs hanging out of 'em and the all-important earful of music coming through the headphones. One of the reasons I like to listen to music out on my runs is the whole observation of life to music. To stare at life with a backdrop of music is really moving. Like many of us, I've sat in a car, stuck in traffic in somewhere you wouldn't think is overly romantic. Then the right music comes on and you just sit and stare and watch people getting on with the same old thing

It all becomes quite poetic. It gives you an appreciation of what we're all up to and where we're all going. Try watching people greet each other in the street to a background of Vivaldi or the old man doffs his cap to the lady across the street to the sound of Frank Sinatra singing my way, beautiful.

Obviously, the escape, ironically, had to involve London, I know, I'm including something I want to get away from in the plan of getting away from it. Not only for the Knowledge (damn thing) but also because it's the best bloody city in the world. As they say in certain media circles, I thought this idea had legs. I'll run around the board I thought. I've seen many of 'Monopoly' pub crawls but none of them ever go the full way around the board and here's the showstopper.... In the order of which they come on the Monopoly board itself. Eh? Escape? That'll do it.

Looking at the board and looking at the map of London I soon realised that there was no way this was a fun 'run' this had to be a fun 'ride'. Looking at it, it had to be done on a bike rather than on my legs. It all looked very colourful. I looked at the pieces you play with, The boat, The Scottie dog, etc. I checked that I had a good enough bike to get round. I checked my clothing; I checked the time and date I'd do it but the one thing that I couldn't get away from was the course. Basically, Monopoly is a geographical nightmare. If you start at 'GO', you go from the Old Kent rd. to Whitechapel and then onto Kings cross station. Up the road to angel, and then it starts to niggle at your mind. You then come back down the hill of Pentonville rd. to get to Euston station. Then back up the hill to Pentonville rd. In fact, this being just yards away from another square on the board, but you can't go there yet. It's such a mind play. The more I looked at it, the more of a challenge it looked like being. I had to concentrate on drawing up my route from one square to the next. And, what place I would call the Waterworks and Electric company. This was certainly what I needed. Over the next couple of weeks, I spent my time planning the route, telling friends, and getting in touch with the NSPCC for a few sponsorship forms. Although this was for personal rejection therapy, I might as well scrape up a few quid for a charity I've always held dear.

I decided I would ride the course wearing a top hat as befitting one of the pieces of the game. Good idea, but I didn't own a top hat. I approached a tailor's in Canary Wharf, just downstairs from my work, and told them all about the bike ride. They thought it was a great idea and duly measured me up for a well fitted hat on the proviso that I returned it as soon as I got off the saddle. Friends at work had a bit of a chuckle about it all and family and close friends just thought I was a little bit silly but all in all I kept everyone at bay over the complete disappointment I felt at being slung back to 56-day appearances.

Once again, I got the local Canary Wharf newspaper 'The Wharf' involved in a little bit of publicity. You can imagine, they loved it, since they knew me from the 'Bridge' run and must have thought that the local crazy has returned but wearing a top hat. It's the kind of stuff local journalists dream of.

The newspaper wanted me to bring my bike to work one day for a few pictures 'Oh and bring the top hat' the guy said over the phone. So, there I was, suit on for work, holding my push bike, wearing my top hat, while taking instructions from the local rag photographer. 'one more holding the hat in the air, that's it, nice big smile' he instructed. Right in the middle of Canada Square. I didn't go to lunch around the area for a few weeks after the embarrassment of 'the shoot'. Anyway, sponsorship was coming along leaps and bounds. Friends at the bank dug deep, family dug a little deeper and I sat and went over and over the course with Jeff as he had volunteered to drive around in his works van with the spare bike on board just in case. I don't know what we were both expecting, we were treating it like the tour de France. Jeff said at one point, I'll have a banana and orange juice ready for you after the first stage, we both fell about laughing.

I'd chosen a Saturday morning. Early enough to get it out the way and all that. The newspaper said that failing any cats being stuck up trees I'd have the whole back page come the Monday morning after the ride. If there was one thing I didn't need while trying to get this Knowledge done it was fame. I console myself with the fact that the total readership of local newspapers has never been the cause of international fame so I was safe in the fact that I wouldn't be sharing a red carpet with George Clooney anytime soon.

Saturday morning came a little quicker than I hoped. I'd typed out the course with little hints of how to get to the next place easy enough. I put on my specially made Monopoly run t-shirt. Jeff on the end of the phone complaining about the state of the flower delivery van and warning me to not be surprised, if we swap bikes halfway around, not to find the top of a couple of tulips sticking out of the saddle.

So, I was off to meet Jeff in the flower van and start the ride on the Old Kent Road. I'd arranged to meet the newspapers photographer at the top of Caledonian rd. later that afternoon to take a couple of pictures outside Pentonville Prison (no collecting two hundred pounds, go straight to jail, boom boom). A lovely day taking my time but keeping an eye on my little milometer that I'd strapped to the handlebars.

Starting in the Lidls car park, at the top of the Old Kent Road, was no glamourous start but now I was underway it was fantastic. Builders in Old Street laughing at my top hat but because of the t-shirt stating what I was up too I was spared the complete grilling. People in Oxford Street not even noticing a man wearing shorts, a colourful t-shirt and a top hat on a bike riding up to Marble arch then back to Liverpool Street. I was up and down all over the place. The Waterworks was the old water board in Rosebury Avenue. Stations took care of themselves. The whole course was geographically stupid. Jeff duly met me at one of the stops along the way with said orange juice, banana, and a collection of goodies to munch down before getting back on the saddle.

As on the Monopoly board, I'd just ticked of Park Lane and joked to myself that the next square along, Super Tax, was being paid by most of the residents of Mayfair. So, I could tick that square of too. With Jeff parked in Queen Street Mayfair, waiting for my sweaty return, I checked the milometer at the end of a fun, and quite uplifting day, to see it read eighty-one kilometres. Again, Jeff had been shopping and greeted me with more orange juice and another banana, he was nothing if not predictable. The photos for the paper came out well. Full back page with some idiot on a bike waving a top hat like a gleeful racehorse owner. All the sponsors paid up and a cheque was sent to the NSPCC to help with the good work for the kids. All in all, a good idea that seemed to do many a different job. A bit of fun around London. A good old work out for my cloudy brain and money for the charity.

I'm looking at the man in the mirror.

I needed to change how I did all this Knowledge. I needed a plan that worked. Other Knowledge boys were getting this thing done in two and a half to three years (admittedly full time but none the less). I'd always known that a Knowledge school is the usual route that most students go. I never felt the usual intimidation of not knowing anyone, or any inferior feeling, I just never really organised my life and convictions enough to go or find out about going to a regular school. I suppose I made the fatal mistake of thinking because the appearances were just you on your own, I thought I could do the study just on my own, a massive mistake. I'd started to look around at some of the possible knowledge schools. I came in from Highams Park in the East so to consider going regularly to one of the oldest and well-established schools, Knowledge point in Caledonian road, would just not be possible in the long run. Clapham Manor Street, green badge school was out of the question and the newly started Cabology school in Redbridge had just closed after quite a short period. I'd known Wizzan in Bow for many a year. Dean Warringtons fresh and clear ideas of how to do the knowledge were quite revolutionary at the time and now he'd branched out into a fully operational school. I thought I'd pop along one night after work. Wizann was only a few stops on the Docklands Light railway from Canary Wharf so wouldn't take up too much time after a long day, pretending, I knew about banking.

And then there was light.

I would be late home that night just going to see what they get up to as if not pinning my every hope on what a Knowledge school could give me. I got off at All Saints DLR station and walked up Chrisp street. Left in Yeo street and there stood about fifty knowledge bikes in the car park of a small trading estate. A few of the smokers were outside and as I passed them near the entrance, I could hear all the conversation evolved around Knowledge. 'Nah, you wouldn't go that way unless the Strand was chokka' I could already feel myself wanting this. I walked in and, not always the case, Dean Warrington, owner, proprietor and general all round Knowledge whiz kid was there on the desk to answer all my 'beginner' questions. With a policy of matching up people of the same standard and not leaving the matching up to the individuals, like a dating agency for call over partners, everything was very welcoming to the newcomer. I'd found my school. I promised myself that I'd get there at least twice a week, some of the full timers would spend all week there and only go out weekends. The work done inside the schools was almost better than seeing the actual places as you got so much more done.

You could call over two hundred different problems, turn arounds and points in a session when you would never be able see that much in a day on your bike. Some of those on the latter stages of 21's had even stopped going out on their bikes as they had literally seen it all and now just concentrated on playing around with knowledge in road and route puzzles up the school. I skipped home feeling that the visit to a Knowledge school was most probably the biggest turning point in the last three years and then slumped into a self-damming tirade of how stupid I'd been not to sign up earlier to a school that could help me so much. To think, these guys in the school were getting to practice hundreds more Knowledge problems by bouncing off one another each day than I had done all week. I'd even heard once at another Knowledge school that a fight broke out at their Christmas party as one Knowledge boy disagreed with another about the Catford one way system. What goes on in school should stay in school. My first proper visit to the school was a few days later and I couldn't have had more of a boost. I'd nearly called the whole appearance sheet with another fella, Mickey Harrington, who didn't seem too bad. If you went to make yourself a cup of tea you would overhear two or three questions on your way 'can you do a left into Oxford Street from there? I'd pop to the toilet and hear the three roads that ran around the Catford one way system. It was hitting me at all angles. All this going on and the time to my 'comeback' appearance was getting closer and closer. I felt like the first couple of appearances on the way back would be a breeze especially with the help of the school behind me. Work at the bank was warming up too. I had to keep up the pretence that I wanted to progress within the organisation and therefore be in line for better pay rises etc to keep the bills being paid. As with all roles, responsibility also came with this as they usually want their pound of flesh for the extra few quid. There I was, pretending to want to go further in banking and there they were pretending they were trying to see me succeed. All they were doing was trying to get another muppet to shoulder the work and all I was doing was trying to get a Green Badge. The whole thing was a game. I'd sneak out of work bang on the contracted five o'clock. Off I'd go to the Knowledge school and fill my head with points, lines, and general London information. Sometimes I was making it three times a week.

The return of the.... Spatial Cowboy

I felt by now, with my continued attendance at the Knowledge school, I stood a great chance of scoring upon my return. With two lots of 56-day appearances, two lots of 28-day appearances under my belt only the cruellest of beings wouldn't see I'd been through hell already. I'm not saying I wanted charity but come on, I'd done three and a half years at this so far. Even if all went well, mathematically, it would still be another year and a half with 56's 28's and the suburbs to do. I must just say at this point, all this to become a London cab driver.

On the morning of my 'comeback' I got ready in plenty of time. I had the shave of my life and my suit looked like I'd borrowed it from James Bond. If my Knowledge was rubbish I deserved the three points on appearance alone. Alas the scoring system just doesn't work that way. I arrived early and saw that the bike parking bay was almost full. I parked right on the edge of the bay knowing it was tight but any other knowledge boys getting their bike would understand the need for space and avoid the dreaded Islington Council traffic warden. Dutch teetered on the edge of the bike bay as I pulled off my helmet and put my gloves in the back of my Rickman top box. Deep breath and in I walked. I booked in and sat down in the waiting room. The pre-exam nerves started to rumble when Mr O'Connor appeared at the door and said clearly, Mr Syme? O'Connor? couldn't they have given me a more forgiving examiner on my return? I followed him into his office and as he asked me to take a seat. I could feel an almost enlightening feeling sitting down. I felt bright and alert. A mixture of knowledge and calm.

He didn't even flick through the file, it was already open, he knew he had an injured soldier on his hands. Public Carriage Office to London Bridge station. Once the left was done onto Pentonville Road it's straight all the way, just the wind in your hair to consider. He was patching up some of my wound's god bless him. Paddington Station to The Dorchester hotel. Bayswater road and Park Lane. I was starting to feel we could be friends after the war. Finally, he said, 'what about, Liberty's to Soho square' in an obvious ploy for me to call the 'dirty dozen'. The dirty dozen being the string of roads that lead you underneath Oxford St. heading east from Regent St. Out they poured Great Marlborough, Noel, Berwick, D'arbly Wardour, Hollen, Gt Chapel, Fareham, Dean, Carlisle and into Soho Sq. Not Quite the full twelve, Omitting Sutton row at the end but a fine set of calling you'll agree. I wanted to quickly tell him of the yearly celebration of the life of Kirsty McColl, where friends, relatives and fans gather around the memorial, in the square, to sing in memory of her. As the line in the song goes 'there's an empty bench in Soho square'. A poignant reminder for me on a day when it was all coming together. O'Connor said something like 'keep going'. With my three points slotted on my withered old score card I booked out. Taking time to reflect in a misty haze as I left the Carriage Office, I gave a little time to the points collectors on the door. I knew they wouldn't take my appearance seriously as a real 56-day test if I told them the history leading up to it. I told them anyway. Long slog blah blah. I think I saw one collector even have his eye on the daily newspaper as I reeled off my three easy runs. They knew it was a given into the next stage. I knew too but I'll take 'em anyway they come.

I strolled up to Dutch and opened the top box to get the gloves out when I noticed a parking ticket on the front under one of my left-over bulldog clips. I looked down and saw the bike was just on the white line of the bay. If I was in a more cynical frame of mind, I might have thought that someone has added a bike into this line and pushed me on the end of sixty quid. I blamed Islington council. They are ferocious when it comes to spotting a parking misdemeanour. I swallowed the sixty quid. I had three points. I rode home thinking of the one thing you deprive yourself of before any exam.... food, warm, big, food.

Nice n easy my man, nice n easy

Life was on full repeat now. A fair bit of family. A bit of work. Lots of Knowledge school. My second 56. I sat in front of Courtney. Again, he could see previous pain had been endured on my little face and took a gentle approach to me. Mainly West End runs and one long Kenwood House in Hampstead to Selfridges which, on closer inspection, proved to be almost straight. So, without delay and a great big smile Courtney whipped my file closed and said, 'now you have six points Mr Syme'. Brilliant. I got a small feeling of what some of these students feel when all goes according to plan. Exactly how it should go when you're in the zone, bang! Three points bang! Six points, bring it on. By this time, I'd started to get to know some of the faces up the Knowledge school. Little did I realise at the time but some of those faces I be saying hello to in many years' time. Some would become very good friends.

I told everyone at the school my story and filled them in being on six and flying. Nice to have a few supporters on the road you travel and, as we were all in the same boat, that support was greatly needed. My work effort greatly improved with my six points and, with any niggly problems being sorted out at the school, it was all falling into place. They say time flies when you're having fun and no truer statement could be said as I realised that my next appearance was quickly approaching.

When you go somewhere for the first time you feel inexperienced, wide eyed and wondering you're young with innocence. After you'd been to that same place hundreds of times you feel the place has become part of you. You can get the feeling that you've come from innocence to maturity in that very place. A bond forms and you can get all melancholy. That was my feeling now thinking of the famous number fifteen Penton St.

Just a smile?

There it was. My third appearance on this lot of 56 day. I walked in the reception area on the ground floor and realised that I'd done this routine so many times I would almost now automatically walk straight to the locked door waiting for the desk staff to flick the switch and wait for the door to click open allowing me upstairs. I'd always have my booking form in my hand just in case but since I'd been coming through those doors now for about four years, I thought at least they could remember my sorry looking face. I booked in, used the facilities, and went into the waiting room. It was packed. A busy one. Names being called so fast that there was almost no time to realise that I'd only been there five minutes when mine was called. I looked up and there she stood. Smart grey suit. Arms straight by her side. She didn't need a pen to twiddle to exert any superiority aura, she was already superior. Danvers. Ms, Miss but not ma'am.

I never did find out whether the no ma'am stance was political in any way. I sat down. It was cold in the room. I felt weak. Again, I was at her disposal if she so wished. Manor house station to Gibson Square. The very first run in the history of the Knowledge? Surely, if she's going to bump me up to nine points, at least make some kind of theatre of the appearance don't just give me what a baby could do. Then came the big guns. Mitcham Lane to Old town Clapham, jeez, where did that come from. I think I knew then that I was going to be sent packing.

She re-loaded and hit me with Clapham Park Rd to Larkhall rise SW4. It's short but there's a no right turn into Clapham High St., and that's the trip wire. I was wounded, she looked over her black rimmed spectacles, and said very slowly, 'take me from Heaven(!) to The Hoist'. Heaven, the famous gay club near Embankment tube station to the very famous S&M dungeon club in Vauxhall. I doubted this was a proposal. My card came back. She didn't say a word. She wrote something on my file, and I'd lost out. Still six points but, now out in the sunshine, I started to warm up and shrug off that strange cold feeling I'd just experienced in the company of the ice lady.

Every now and again I would view this strange existence I had of studying the Knowledge while keeping it a secret from work mates and bosses at work. My life could be in absolute turmoil some days through the Knowledge and I'd walk into the office like nothing else was going on with me. I was occasionally impressed by my standard of acting out this parallel life. Although, I could never really hear the sentence 'And the next award for best acting corporate employee goes to… 'I'd just like to thank Honda for making such a reliable machine. Dutch was always reliable. My mate Jeff would often bang on to me about maintenance, and silly little routines I should do to keep her in good shape, but until she starts coughing, everything's fine, isn't it?

Time was moving on at a rate of knots. Now I'd moved to Epping. My route to civilisation consisted of one long road. Through Epping Forest, South Woodford to the A12. Come off at Canary Wharf with just enough time to give you a chapped face. I remember coming through the forest one day and, suddenly, Dutch had a big cough. She shuddered and sputtered and then abruptly cut out. I was doing about thirty miles an hour at the time and luckily, with no one behind me, I had to screech to a halt at the side of the road. After getting off and checking it out, which consisted of me just taking off my helmet and bending slightly towards the engine and then realising I wouldn't know what I was looking for even if it had a bell on it. I kick started her once and she responded well. I left her running for a few minutes and promised to run her into a bike shop the next time I was passing.

Mr Wilkins. The re-match

I was confident right up until my name was called. Mr Wilkins. I must have been a right rascal in a past life to deserve all this. As I walked out of the waiting room, I swear I could hear a snigger from one of the Knowledge boys sitting down. I checked my flies which is always the best course of action when hearing unexpected laughter. It must have been a nervous reaction as they realised it wasn't them destined for the east London wizard. 'Morning Mr Syme' he said all robust and cheerily. I replied thinking if you're going to kick me in the crown jewels, could you do it now as I'm close to the door and wouldn't have so far to crawl out the room.

He opened my file. Silence. Then he said, 'I know you know where the Armourers Hall is, but do you know a good umbrella shop?' Only one sprang to mind. The famous Smith Bros. on New Oxford Street. 'Away you go then'. I finished calling the run and he said, 'Cleopatra's needle, no one seems to know that all the chippings around the base were caused by German planes during the Blitz of London in the second world war'.

He stopped, looked out the window and continued. 'They all know it's four and a half thousand years old, but they don't know what happen sixty years ago'. He seemed saddened by the general public's lack of knowledge on such matters. For some reason, I felt guilty.

'Take me from the shrapnel marks of the needle to where Texas gained its independence'. Pickering place, SW1 St James's. I blurted it out. I knew that he was impressed that I didn't even flinch at the independence thing. He now must know that I've read a little about the place as well as throwing petrol in 'ol Dutch. 'Last one' he said, as if I'd done alright so far and the pain would soon end. 'Do you know where I would have got my badge' referring to his age and where the old carriage Office was in Lambeth Road. 'mm, you're guessing my age now aren't you?'. Then, strange, but I thought I could see a smile emerging from under that bushy moustache. Either a smile or the moustache had started to grow in front of my very eyes. 'You're right, I don't look it do I?' he was enjoying this, and I felt all the nerves and tension just ease away in the company of what I thought was now my new uncle from east London. 'Get me up to here in a straight line and you're done for the day' he said pointing to his office. Lambeth road to Penton Street. All I had to do was get this straight and he's virtually told me I'll be on nine points looking for my drop to 28's. I was out of breath when I'd finished but they seemed big enough roads to re check in my mind as I called them to know it was good. I looked at his face as he gave my card back and the moustache was now broad with kindness. Although not really the done thing, I shook his hand. Let bygones be bygones. I know this was the man who put me back by about three years but, today, he was Uncle Wilkins. The spluttering problem with Dutch was slowly getting worse. Like knowing there's a serious illness but not wanting to acknowledge it. I started to realise that maybe Jeff was right, and I should have kept an eye on the oil. I don't think it was particularly promising that I one day asked Jeff 'What is that watering can sign with a little drop coming out of the top'. Jeff still remembers that day I enquired about the oil and that little red sign. I topped her up with oil and all seemed well for now but, again, I was just looking the other way.

Three times a week Knowledge school. Work was asking for a little more effort from all the departments on our floor and I'd run out of things to run or cycle round so the Knowledge, as usual, was all encompassing.

Mrs Sadlier

I remember that first appearance when I walked in with my full-length coat on and Mrs Sadlier, knowing it was my first time, politely asking me to leave my coat on the hook outside next time. Funny, I was so fresh to all this then.

She asked me to sit down. She had a little chat and she looked truly concerned about my path and why it had been so rocky for me. I felt she really wanted to know. I poured out my heart in the fashion of seeing a counsellor. I nearly came out with 'Nobody understands me' but thought this might send a wrong message or, worse, grate on her nerves. I remained polite and tried to compose myself and I didn't want to fall for the wolf in sheep's clothing act. 'Goldman Sachs', she said. I thought I know where they are, but they don't have a sign on the wall. You're always trying to find the hidden agenda before you answer the question, and this was an indication of a D in the offering if I messed up. This wasn't a push over, rightly so, as I was looking for my drop to 28's with this appearance. 'To the Iveagh bequest blue plaque'. Crikey, she's trying to not score me. I had to be right up on my game for this one. These were tricky points. 'Can you take me from the stage door of the dominion theatre to the Palladium theatre'. Blimey, I'm hanging on to threads here. The stage door? it's around the corner in Bainbridge St. and tricky to turn around for the straight line on Oxford St. I sensed the kind old lady baking rock cakes had gone. I was face to face with the grey cardigan killer.

Now my mind is racing. I'm ready to run out the door if this gets physical. 'Ok, what about Spring St to Euston station' delivered with a smile. No right turn at the top of Spring St. so you've got to use Conduit mews to continue your way. My palms were clammy. I could have cooked sausages under my armpits. Suddenly I found that I was getting through quite a tough appearance. I felt like the Special Forces when all communications are down and nothing's going according to plan, they still plug on. Survival was key. Crash, I'd called three tough ones and then, breathing in and out in a controlled manner she hit me with a fourth run. The fourth run? The fourth run never comes out unless they're not happy or they're just confirming a decision they've already made. 'Chelsea Gate, Battersea to Edinburgh Gate please' she said, like she had just pulled a tray of roasted potatoes out of the oven. They say beware of sweet honey offered on a sharp knife and this appearance had now taken a nasty turn. My eyes narrowed as I thought of that wolf in sheep's clothing. I'd been tricked. This was Luke Skywalker versus Lord Vader. I'd done my best. Maybe she wanted to hold me back one last time, but she had no option. She scored me. Hallelujah! Weeeeeee. My drop to 28's. Champagne will get drunk. A dance or two will be had, and love is in the air…Hold on Dutch, we're nearly there.

Let's have a little look at things here. The newly acquired house in the sleepy suburb of Epping was now nearing completion on the decoration front. I was a regular at the Wizann knowledge school which meant occasionally someone would offer to make me a cup of tea as I walked in and started to de-robe. Work seemed to be stable, and the social life had started to pick up at the same time as my mood. I was busy but very aware that my first 28-day appearance of this second time around, was just around the corner.

Mr Jenkins – no truer word spoken.

Nothing ever goes according to plan in this life so it's nice to hear all the real bumps and grinds of what the books don't tell you. Someone who was practicing the teaching was Mr Jenkins. 28's eh? this was the big time. Knowledge boy myth had it that 28's was where they really tested you. At 56's they're just slapping you into shape. On 21's you've done all the hard work. 28's was where they tested your metal. I followed Mr Jenkins down to his office. I could already feel this was going to be a lively appearance as Jenkins never held back a view or, for the matter, toned down the volume when making it. 'Right, take a seat, let's give this a go' he said, already upping the volume. I smiled to myself thinking this kind of approach to an exam would never happen at a refined public school. I just imagined a pupil being asked by one of the Eton lecturers 'right Smithers, you think you know about Philosophy, well let's 'ave some Descartes then'. 'Undershaft' he said and didn't even look up. As I fumbled through my thoughts of where that was or what it even meant he said, 'to The Insurers Hall'. I was just stunned. He waited for my mind to crawl up into a ball and said' come on, you're with the big boys now'. 'Sorry Sir' was all I could offer. It's never too encouraging when someone starts a sentence with oh my god but Jenkins then said 'oh my god, St Mary Axe then to Basinghall st'. This is obviously where the first two points were but it's too late now. He hit me with a couple more while saying things like 'how do you expect to get this badge when you can't even answer these ' cos you'll get asked these out there' as he pointed to the world outside the window. He wrote something on my card. I hoped it was a little message to the next examiner to take it easy on me next time because I've been smashed to bits today. 'Oi' he said, again the public-school analogy plonked into my head, 'I suggest you have a word with your family and tell 'em you're moving into the knowledge school full time, see if they can help you with sleeping arrangements'. It was humorous but only in retrospect. I suppose I should have expected a no score on this first one just to get me to pull my socks up. I had to remind myself that this was all to drive a cab and thought it strange that at the end of all this I still wouldn't be a brain surgeon or lawyer. I'm sure their study isn't so erratic.

Syme versus Thomas

Grey suit. Immaculate grey hair and a picture behind his desk of himself leaning against a grey sports car. This man loved a bit of grey. I was the only one in the waiting room as we walked to his office. At half eleven in the morning, it was a late appearance, but I was ready for this. I'd got the train down and left Dutch at home as the oil problem started to worry me and thought two coughs a week was now cause for concern.

I had all my sticky lists in my pocket out on the train and fully rehearsed them on the way. By the time I sat down I was ready to look Mr Thomas in the eye.

'They sell some nice cars, Lamborghini, don't they?' he said. Whoa, I know he likes cars so now I'm racking my brains for everything related to cars in London. I'm thinking of Kwik Fit in Delancey st. I thought of the Blue Bird restaurant in Kings Road, as this was the biggest car garage in Europe way back in the twenties. My brain went car crazy. The run turned out to be the Lamborghini showroom in Old Brompton Rd (or OBR, as it's called in the trade) to the Royal Oak taxi centre under the flyover at Paddington. I done that and he didn't say a word. 'Pelham Crescent to Blakes hotel'. It's all south Kensington and I'm getting them straight away. He's got to be impressed. He's not even waiting for me to call out where the first point is.

He assumes I've got a bit of history with South Ken hence how quickly I'm calling these out. Blakes hotel? it's only round the corner but I'll take these points anyway they come. 'Highgate West Hill to Jacksons Lane' he said with a wry smile that said I'd fallen for his South Kensington trap. Gulp! Right at the very top of north London. Testing the six-mile boundary.

This was proper north London. This was far enough north for a weekend away in the summer. I took my time. I was pleased with the first two runs and thought I'd use a little bit more time trying to crack this hilly nightmare. Silence. He started to write. Now, if there's one thing, I know that's, if they don't start telling you how rubbish you've been and asking you what's going wrong with your study then you've scored. He raised his head and said, 'how long you been doing this now? years isn't it?'. Admittingly, he wasn't making me feel too good but he's doing the old, have a go at him but then hand the card over and make him feel like he's got away with something trick. He was nodding his head like he doesn't know anyone who's taken so long to get this done but he knows as well as I do that there's plenty of part time knowledge boys who are racking up years while trying to get their badge, so the psychological play wasn't going to affect me at all. 'Well, at least you're on your way now' he said still with a look of bemusement on his face.

He handed back my card as if I'd got sticky honey all over it. I must admit, the same piece of battered card no bigger than a decent bookmark was sure to look a bit bedraggled, but he didn't have to look at it like it was something to do with a personal hygiene problem. Three points on 28's.

Now I was doing so well in my mind I could talk about it with family and friends. It's advisable to start booking things like your cab driving test. Getting practical things like good garages to rent from. Or look to see if you took the plunge and bought a cab at this stage, so as when you get up to six or nine points on 28's you were ready to go. I found this practical stuff breath taking. This was about the real doing of the job. This wasn't calling over or feeling like you're in Grand Turismo with the wind going through your hair, this was about the actual job.

Syme versus Price…. Nice Price

Five minutes in that Knowledge waiting room can feel like a lifetime. You can feel the tension. You can see in the eyes of your fellow sufferers their anxieties or their confidence. The ever-present gigantic map on that wall shows you the whole of London on a massive scale. The size of the map reminds you that you've accumulated more Knowledge about this city than the majority of ordinary folk will ever have the privilege to know about this city. If anyone dared speak in that room, they were either mad, nervous, or extremely confident. Sitting there, I had none of these emotions.

I was void of feeling when I heard the gentle creek of brown hush puppies. It seems that these Puppies weren't hushing. Nevertheless, that creek gave me enough time to turn my head to see which examiner was turning the doorway. Mr Price. I need three points here to be halfway through 28's and look who's turned up, Lord Werthers Original himself. The usual cardigan under the suit was worn and not a scratch on the brown shoes, I was in good hands here. I sat down and looked up.

'Do you know Duncannon St.?' he said, as if giving an option that, if I don't know it, he might crack out one that I would. Things were looking up as he asked me from there to the Royal Courts of Justice in the strand. It couldn't have got easier. Then he said, 'well done'. An easy run and a compliment, this man would be on my Christmas card list for a long time to come. 'Well, now I know you know Duncannon st, how about going from there to Harrods'. Well, I can't drop the points at either end but Duncannon st is one way going in the other direction. My next left would be Burliegh st and I'd have to take it through Covent Garden which will make this a bit of a heavy call. Using most of China town and St James's and about seventeen roads later, I arrived at Harrods. He's not a bad guy Mr Price. He wants you to drive a cab. He doesn't want Scientists. He wants what the punters want, the West End. 'Let's have a few theatres then'. A few? how many does he want? Do I just start calling out theatres I know? 'Take me from Her Majesty's and drop off at the Apollo and then stop outside the Arts theatre' he said constantly writing in my file. Sometimes I'd forgotten mid-run where I was actually heading to, but this man had seen all that before.

I finished calling in great Newport St with the Arts theatres on the left. I'd got 'em. I knew I'd got 'em. He gave me back my card as I stood up and said, 'well done, keep going'. I took back my card and he'd held on slightly too long or I pulled too early and wallop, the card split in half. 'Lucky that weren't my sleeve' he said with a friendly smile. I thought, come on Mr Price, they sell those cardigans in the army supply shops. Those cardigans are made to last. I could've pulled his arm out of its socket before pulling the sleeve of that little tweed number.

Halfway through 28's. Four more appearances to score just twice. I'm sad to say but it looked like the dinner plate steering wheel on the cushion was soon to be discarded for the real thing. I would no longer pretend that my sofa was the cab and my dinner plate, with a picture of some beach in Cornwall, was the steering wheel. The kitchen as the West End and my bathroom as the City were soon to be replaced by real London. It was all getting serious.

DUTCH R.I.P

I remember it well. It was a cold start to the day. Saturday, and I'd planned all my work out. I was out to get around thirty points and look at the one-way system at the top of Streatham high road. I got dressed in my usual outfit. Balaclava under my helmet. Good thick gloves, that were no good for anything but keeping your hands warm, and my waterproof bike jacket that I'd owned since the day I'd started the knowledge when me and Jeff walked into Johns scooters and said, 'dress me for the long haul'. Alas, my waterproof bike trousers were now looking much worse for wear. I'd taken to cellotape around the bottom of the left leg and the right leg was so ripped to shreds that it reminded me of a bloke at the knowledge school whose clothes were in the same condition, and they called him the Lion tamer.

I kick started Dutch into life and headed off out of Epping into the forest. As I reached halfway through the forest near the Wake Arms roundabout, poor old Dutch cough and spluttered all in one go and completely gave up the ghost. She'd had a massive engine attack. I would later find out the cause of death would be contributed to 'owner negligence'. By all accounts, the one thing that Honda stipulate, for the engine to last a lifetime, was regular oil changes. I'd killed my Knowledge partner and there was no penalty to pay apart from guilt. She had forty-two thousand miles on the clock. Not bad for a pizza delivery bike. I wonder if it had been used to deliver pizza's, how many Hawaiians would have been dished out on that kind of milage. Forty-two thousand miles of London covered in circles and strange patterns. The poet in me looked around the forest that fateful day and thought forty-two thousand miles of hope. A tear made its way down my cheek and then a Greggs delivery van drove through a puddle and soaked my right-hand side. I decided to move over to a layby. I got Dutch home and lay her in wake in the garage waiting for the day when the spare parts undertaker would take her away. I felt guilty arranging to get a new bike, but she'd understand that our magnum opus was about to be achieved.

After a couple of weeks of searching, I was offered a bike free of charge by an ex-Knowledge boy, and friend, Martin. We agreed that I could finished the Knowledge on his old bike, which wasn't that old, but at the end I would be given the job of selling it and passing the proceeds on to him. It was a good deal for me. One thing I didn't really think to ask was about the power of the bike. It was a 50cc which in layman's terms meant that I'd often be overtaken by cocky milkmen in their floats and power walkers would be blowing raspberries from the side of the road but beggars can't be choosers.

Mr Syme versus Mr Field

I'd had the 'new' bike for about two weeks. Which meant, with a 50cc under my backside, I'd barely seen above thirty-four miles an hour and there was never a wind blowing through my hair. Nevertheless, I'd done a bit of work and I'd been a regular up the school, so confidence was on my side.

On the day of this appearance, I decided to get the tube down to the carriage office as I'd heard on the weather report that a north easterly wind would be blowing that morning and didn't feel that the little 50 could push through in time for my 8.45am appearance. I tried to do a little revision on the train but, what with the drift of late commuters and hustle and bustle of early morning travel, thought it best to just sit and observe. Nice and early in the booking hall gave me time to let dust settle. As I washed my hands at the row of sinks in the gents, I noticed the Knowledge boy next to me, who'd obviously seen youth pass him by a good few years ago, was splashing a little aftershave on. Aftershave? what did he think they were looking for? John Travolta and a good understanding of discos in South London? I followed 'J.T' out and we both took our seats as a couple of the others waiting raised their noses. I saw one fella put his head down and smile. Obviously, the seventies aroma that J.T had splashed on had reminded him of a lucky holiday in the sunshine or, he thought the same as me and didn't think this was a chance to lead the examiners into an aromatic trance. As the aroma filled the air, I'm sure we were all thinking the same thing by wanting to be called in first as there was a good chance of suffocation.

Mr Field swung around the door, and I was first. Saved from dying from inhaling strong alcohol-based colognes, I was on my way to battling for nine points on 28's. Just thinking I could come out of this room with nine points on 28's was enough to make my legs go weak. Thankfully, I sat down just as the strength was about to go.

As usual, he was bright, cheery, and red faced. We went through a few niceties and then it was down to business. To be honest, he was a bit like Mr Price. They don't want to trick you; they want to know you could get people around as a cab driver. He asked me, politely, to take him from the Rotherhithe Tunnel, on the south side, to where Oswald Mosley and his fascist black shirts were defeated in battle. Culling circus to Cable Street. All went well and then he threw in the MI6 building in Vauxhall to the MI5 building. Only by chance I remember that James Bond once had an office in Thames House on Millbank for the MI5, so I jumped for that. Correct. I called it while trying to hide my surprise that Ian Fleming and James Bond had just helped me out on 28's.

One more and, again, no real problems and if this goes along the lines of the normal, call three and you're out, then I'm in for nine points here. The

London Palladium to the secret garden inside Regents Park. I mean, it's secret and you're not meant to know where it is. I knew where it was and so does half of North London. I also knew that it backed onto the only private residence in the inner circle of Regent's Park, thanks to Jeff telling me the Sultan of Brunei being the owner. I didn't think that now was the time to ask Mr Field whether he knew that, so I just called the run. 'Have you booked your drive?' he said while writing on my now ripped and cellotaped card. 'Erm' was all I could muster as he passed me back my card and then said, 'well, I think you'd better do that soon'. Nine points, 28's. four and a half years. A round or two was bought for the chaps at work, who were none the wiser of the reason for my generosity. A few packets of biscuits were bought for the Knowledge boys and girls up the school, which pleased my friend Jim, as we joked, he was no stranger to a buffet. As they sing in a certain Disney film, 'Zipiddy do dar, zippidy day, I've got nine points and I'm on my way'……. or something like that.

Not Mrs but Mr Sadlier

Eddie Sadlier, the husband of Mrs Sadlier the examiner. A chain smoking, fast talking, do a deal, Irishman. A real nice, down to earth, fella who was part of the real world rather than the walled castle that is the P.CO. I suppose there were other options to book your cab driving lessons, but Eddie was the main man that everyone went to and, at this stage, I wasn't rocking any boat or trying to be individual in anyway. See, they get you to conform in the end. I rang Eddie and, through a tirade of words, he arranged my first three driving lessons with more to come once I got in the swing of things. Meeting Eddie for my first lesson over in the east London paradise of Ilford was like meeting an ancient mythical figure.

I stood on the corner of a quiet residential street when, surrounded by mist, appeared a figure. Short, round, with messy curly hair that would make any barber wince. With a hint of facial hair and clothes that were just worn to do a job. Trousers with good pockets to keep a roll of bank notes in. A V neck jumper that had seen better days and shoes you could've done a paper round in.

The mist wasn't the low-lying cloud of a weather torn Ilford but rather the smoke from his thirteenth cigarette that morning. Like a jazz singer reaching for the mike, he held out his hand and warmly greeted me. A lovely man. You knew were you stood with Eddie as soon as you met him. Within no time he'd given me the rundown of all the knobs and buttons inside the cab, and we were off along the mean streets of IG1. Eddie, shouting instructions in the back, like a paying passenger, and me, at the helm, like I knew what I was doing. The public would have just seen a cab driver and a punter. Little did they know that if anything other than straight ahead was needed I would be scuppered.

It went well enough. I'd done about an hour when we drew up to where we met. Eddie gave me a lot of confidence because he spoke clearly, asked straight forward questions, and refused to stop smoking throughout our time together. The man was a walking biology experiment. Eddie lit cigarette number nineteen and drove off with the local fire brigade in hot pursuit. I'd got that lesson under my belt and really felt like I was heading away from office life and into a different kind of existence. That strange realisation would rear its head every now and again. No boss, no employees, no premises as such. No fixed working hours. Just me and London. My next driving lesson with Eddie would be just after my next appearance.

Syme versus Courtney

Things were moving at a pace that I couldn't control. I'd had my first cab driving lesson, so now I knew how things felt behind the wheel. I also knew that the steering wheel was slightly bigger than my dinner plate. And further knew that, compared to Martins little 50cc, Dutch was a Ducati.

I'd made friends up the knowledge school, Jim, Mickey, Frazer and all those other faces that I'd one day see out there with a raise of the eyebrow or show of a finger. Their support, and ribbing, was part of the network that had pushed me to the edge of the big time, well, 21's, if you can call that the big time. I faced Courtney for my drop. Let me just say that again. I faced Courtney for my drop to 21's. 21's? what was I doing here? I remembered the saying up the school that when you go up the Carriage Office you always know more than you think but 21's? surely not. As usual, Courtney was the epitome of Caribbean style. Grey suit with wide open jacket and, although he wore a tie, you hardly noticed it as he was always so free and easy with his swagger. I'd heard over the past few weeks that Courtney had had enough of being mister nice guy and wanted to make sure that anyone he let through to 21's really did know their London. Gulp. Was I to see the new, improved, Mr Courtney? Or was I to be scorched by his fiery tongue?

He asked me Bonnington Square in Vauxhall. Famous for the squatter's invasion where most of the, then, dilapidated square was occupied by a whole squatting community.

After years of negotiation and legal battles the squatters won the right to reside in the Square's beautiful Georgian houses. Can you imagine that nowadays? Wonderful exotic plants, and a real cool café have flourished in the square since those heady days, creating a unique community and something that is just a credit to people power.

He didn't want to know all that though, he just wanted Bonnington Square to Waterloo station. Easy peasy.. Listen to me, easy peasy. There was a time that would have taken me until next Tuesday to call. Then it was Waterloo station to, as he put it, Charlie Chaplin's old house. Milverton Street in Kennington. I'll always get that one as, growing up in NW5, my block of flats was called Milverton. He was impressed, I could see his broad smile edging through. Mitcham Lane SW17. Hello, I thought, someone's testing someone here. Take him to Nightingale Lane in Clapham. Once upon a time, I would rather have sat in frogspawn than attempt to call this southwest nightmare, but I could see a line through Atkins Road and Cavendish Road. I could see a line in SW17? the planets were conspiring to help me.

I called it like I was possessed by someone who lived off Streatham High rd. I'd backed him into a corner. He couldn't do anything apart from plunge for the 'fourth run'. He didn't. He looked up with a great big, beautiful smile. His teeth were a credit to a mother's strict guidance. He handed back my card and then, like a gift I didn't know was coming, gathered together a load of different paperwork for me to take. A form to book my cab driving test and, would you believe, a brochure of brand-new cabs. All the colours with all the prices. The brochure was mouth-watering. I shook his hand and felt like I'd just been accepted into the fold. 21's. It's past serious now, it's emotional.

Although it was a really miserable day weather wise, I was full of the joys of spring. I'd gone there that day on the snail machine, and I knew I was faced with an extra half hour on my journey back. I didn't mind the weather or the little 50cc doing its best to get me east as there was that big silver lining called 21's.

I'd made it up most of Seven Sisters Road when, just before the station, I see a woman coming out of a side road looking to her left trying to enter the main road. The road was wet and the rain trying to get heavier. I thought surely, she's got to look to her right at any point now but oh no she went for it. Although I was only doing about ten mile an hour, it was still very difficult to stop and, crunch, over her bonnet I went. It seemed like I was in the air for about half an hour but, in those few seconds, I think I'd promised to be good forever, do more charity work and be nice to all living things. The bike flew across the road, and I ploughed straight into the small Turkish supermarket opposite. The owner came running out, the woman in the car ran over and an old lady with her shopping trolley made the sign of the cross on her chest, things weren't good. All I kept thinking to myself was I hoped that my back was OK otherwise there wouldn't be a badge at the end of this rainbow.

The bike seemed fine so there was no point in doing the insurance thing and, after lots of help and one hell of a lively Espresso from the Turkish guys in the shop, I was back on the road thanking my lucky stars how today had turned out. 21's and I'm still alive. I spent nearly three weeks looking through the new cab brochure. I don't think there was a cab on the road in that time that I hadn't looked at. I noticed the drivers, their differing ages, looks of experience and couldn't believe I was on the cusp of joining it all. I had another driving lesson over in Ilford, only this time Eddie handed over the reins to his sidekick John. John, an experienced cab driver, had a few gold rings one of which had on it DAD. I didn't know whether this was a nice gesture from one of his brood or a statement that he was the 'Daddy' of the open prison he looked like he'd just escaped from.

John had shoulder length hair, which he occasionally brushed in front of you.

It looked like the seventies had passed far too quickly for him. I set off to dazzle him with my straight lines and even straighter arms. Again, I did well and was pleased with another hour in a cab and not yet guilty of any bodily harm to any member of the public. John, straight out of the Eddie Sadlier school of motoring, also smoked throughout the lesson. At the end, I felt like a smoked kipper ready for packaging.

Syme versus Mr Dixon

With the amount of work I was now putting into this Knowledge, along with the evenings at the school, calling over, and putting in the physical work, I was, even if I do say so myself, red hot. Obviously, I should have been this good three years before now but nevertheless, I was now at the helm. Taking the little 50cc from home to the Carriage Office was starting to be a thing of the past. The hairdryer was left at home, and I jumped on the Central line and changed at Tottenham Court Road for the Northern line to Angel. Just for practice, in my head, I would be calling all the roads from each station to station as we went along. The idea being of finishing the run before the tube had got to that next station. I was possessed and there was nothing anyone could do about it. You got to remember some have a London map in every room in the house. The most extreme I've heard was the fella who, painstakingly, drew a sprawling map of London all over the walls in his rented flat. As you came into his flat, you would see extremely detailed scribblings over all the walls and, as you went through to the lounge, into the kitchen, the road system would be almost geographically perfect even to the point where, when he had a few spare moments, would even draw little pictures of some of the more notable points, Big Ben and the London Eye etc. Rumour had it that, he also kept two tins of white paint in his cupboard for the time when he got his 'rec', (finished appearances and onto suburbs) to then paint the whole flat back to his landlord's standard, see, deluded but thoughtful. This kind of story made me, and the thousands of other hopefuls, look quite sane. I've never seen Mr Dixon anything but very smart in appearance and exuding an organised manner. Cool and collected, never really showing too much emotion, he asked me to take a seat. There was a silence that I thought I needed to break but held my tongue and sat and sat and sat. He'd silenced me out, so I had to say something. 'I've been working a lot harder over the past few months sir' I said, like I was already pleading for mercy. 'Well, you don't get to this stage any other way' he returned.

I was bracing myself because if there was anything I really needed to know about Dixon, it was that he loved north London and, now I'm on 21's, it would be trickier parts of north London to test my frazzled brain. He wanted the Iveagh Bequest, which is the old stately home, Kenwood House, in Hampstead Lane, donated to the nation by Lord Iveagh when he died in 1927. Parts of the film Notting Hill were filmed there but I think romance was the last thing on Mr Dixons mind as he just wanted me to take him to East

Finchley station. Nice start. Finished that and onto the next. Gospel Oak station, ah, my old route to school at William Ellis, going to The Spaniards Inn, back in Hampstead Lane Opposite the Iveagh Bequest blue plaque. The Spaniards Inn, there can't be more written about this one. The highwayman Dick Turpin would pop in for a pint back in the day. It's been mentioned in Dickens and Bram Stokers Dracula. It was part of the Tollgate to the old entrance to the Bishop of London's estate and it's been said that many a scoundrel would base themselves here as it has a great vantage point, to see far and wide, who would be coming up the hill. It's also one of the loveliest, countrified, pubs in London and well worth tethering up your horse outside. Mr Dixon seemed happy jotting down how I'd done on these two and, with the last one being Jacksons Lane off the archway road to Muswell hill Broadway, he'd virtually given me three points on my first 21-day appearance. I was in a state of being possessed by the Knowledge right now so it would take a real tricky run to knock me off balance. Maybe it was true when they say all the hard work has been done by 21's and they just want you to be realistic at this stage. He smiled at my ragged card, kept together by cello tape, and gave it back to me saying 'it's been a long time'. Three points on 21's. In nine weeks time, I could be getting my rec and, if my driving test is booked close to that time, I could be on my suburbs in just under three months. Let me sit down, breathe, come on Mark, breathe.

My appointment card had a rip right down the middle. It'd had coffee and tea stains all over it. It had a corner chewed off during one of my more nervous appearances. Now though, this battered old piece of card had a line across it signalling 21-day appearances and under that line was the scrawl of Mr Dixon and it said 'C'. That scrawl, and that letter C, made it the most perfect thing to gaze at. I would arrive home and sit down purposely to gaze at my acquired three points. Reflecting on all those other scrawls with a melancholy warmth. I'd use that perfect looking card to cheer myself up. Bad day at work Mark? never mind, look at your card. Foot in a puddle Mark? never mind, look at your card. Trousers rip on a nail? never mind, look at your card. The thing was pure sunshine, and nothing was taking it away. I hear the question, what is art? Well, that old card with all its effort and memories, that was art my friends. I was in love, and no one could tear us apart. Those days of wine and roses are few and far between but, for now, the wine was flowing.

Syme versus Jenkins

Like all good things, the three-point hangover wore off and I could suddenly feel my next 21-day appearance approaching. This is the quick fire round and I'd better be on my game. With just two weeks now until my next one, I knew I'd be on the runway if I could crack in another score. Usual drill applied. Gathering lots of points sheets and calling all the current appearances. I'd become a bit of a Guru down the Knowledge school. I'd got to the dizzy heights, like most long-term Knowledge boys, where I would often be consulted for the final decision in a minor Knowledge dispute or looked upon for words of wisdom, which never came.

Anyway, back to reality. On the day of my appearance, I walked into the foyer of the Carriage Office only to be greeted by a small, concerned, crowd gathered around a poor bloke who'd just fired half his guts into a nearby rubbish bin. The lady behind the front desk hinted that maybe it could be food poisoning when one of the points collectors from outside suggested it's more likely 56-day appearances. While bent double, the poor fella raised his head slightly to correct the collector informing us all that he was on the map test stage. He wasn't even on 56 days. I looked at the collector, who now looked so shocked, as he crossed his chest, in the religious fashion, we both realised this little soldier has an awfully long road ahead if this is how he is at the map.

I'm drumming my fingers on the arm of the chair. I'm sitting in the waiting room when suddenly, a friendly voice says 'nice shoes. In the past five and a half years I have never heard a compliment, not only in the waiting room, the den of nerves, but anywhere on the knowledge apart from, 'yeah, I suppose that's good enough'.

Mr Jenkins. Not again. How many times am I going to meet this man. People will start to talk. Just when I thought I'd be getting a nice comfortable appearance I get, arms a swinging, cor blimey guvnor, I'm a real cab driver, Jenkins. I sit down, after being asked to take a seat obviously, and he looks me up and down. Silence, then 'Trafalgar Square, I know you know where that is, take me to the tomb of the unknown soldier'. Oh, I get it I thought. Big easy point to sneaky, trip you up, point. Well, not today, Mr Jenkins. Straight down to Westminster Abbey I went. The tomb is inside. 'White Tower then to the black museum' he requested. All around parliament square and Victoria today then. I don't mind this as I've always liked it around that SW1 manor. This should be the last one I thought. He's not a man who messes around.

You get three runs from Mr Jenkins and, if you do well, you know you've done well. Here it comes. I waited. 'The old Gatwick express entrance of Victoria station to Chomley Park, come on I ain't got all day' he was blunt but friendly. This run is so long that I'm going to need all day to call it. It's Buckingham Palace Road to Highgate Hill. As I ran out of breath and finished the run, he started writing without saying a word and, I will guarantee you this, Mr Jenkins wouldn't trick you. If you do well, you get your points and when he's quiet and writing, he's only writing two things. One is how well you've just done for the other examiners to read next time round and the second is your score of three points. It went quiet and he wrote and, as he wrote, my eyes filled with what can only be described as...water. Look where I am, six points on 21 days. I've got another driving lesson in the cab in two days' time and by all accounts I've got nice shoes. These are days that need sky plus'ing.

Fast Eddie

Ilford on a Monday morning, God help me. Mind you, there I am thinking of myself when I really should be worried about my driving instructor, chain smoking Eddie. I could see him coming four hundred yards away in a battered old TX1. I stood on the corner of a quiet residential area in Ilford when he turned the corner. Smoke billowing from the driver's window and the faint noise of a chesty cough. He pulled up, what seemed to be, an unusually long hand brake. After a few polite greetings, and a firm shake of the hands, Eddie jumped in the back, and I took my place in the cockpit. Two buttons were missing from the dashboard and the steering wheel had, at some point, been chewed. Yep, chewed!

With Eddie requesting a 'nice, easy slide into drive' I got going on the mean streets of Ilford. I quickly noticed, while crawling along at a snail's pace, before joining the main road, that the speedometer read sixty-four miles per hour.

The intercom didn't work either, leaving Eddie to shout all his instructions with virtually no air left in his lungs. At one point I stopped at a red light. When told to release my foot on the brake and apply the handbrake I realised it was like pulling a snooker cue up to the top of the roof. You needed arms like, well, Eddie to pull this thing up. I assured Eddie that I'd put the handbrake on then, realising that he'd seen the internal locking lights showing, that my foot was still on the brake. Of course, Eddie didn't say a word, not because he was being polite to someone just learning the trade, oh no, it's because the internal locking system didn't work either.

They talk about some cars being Friday night cars. Being so bad due the workers rushed workmanship as it was Friday night, and they want to get off home for the weekend. This cab must have been put together by one hundred disgruntled, soon to retire, under pensioned, mechanics with a grudge against cab drivers. Eddie said the cab had character. He'd always ask me to leave a road when a police car was present.

Overall, the lesson went well. I enjoyed the fact that I had to put up with certain minor faults with the TX1. Adversity can really be a good tutor. I think Eddie traded on adversity when it came to some of the cabs he was teaching in. I paid Eddie on the street corner and chatted to him about my six points and what that all means to me, but he strangely drifted off in the conversation when I pulled out my payment. The man was a businessman. He didn't seem that interested in my six points. More interested in my six fivers. Eddie advised that I should be getting ready for my 'drive' in a few weeks and said, on my next lesson, we'd spend it in a mock test mode. A mock test? Eddie, you know how to thrill a man don't you.?

Syme versus O'Connor

Obviously, I've been a little busy of late, you know, drinking reasonably priced sparkling wine while celebrating said points. Anyway, too busy to take interest in anything but the Knowledge. I can't help feeling a little pang in my heart that my dear old Arsenal have now signed all relevant paperwork to move them from Highbury to their, new soon to be state of the art, Emirates stadium over in Ashburton Grove. The cranes are in full swing, and the scenery is changing around town. As you can see, I was doing my work out there and keeping abreast of significant area changes and particularly the rejuvenation of that part of North London. John Lennon was famously quoted as saying that life is what happens while you're planning other things. Well, John, you were bang on because, at six points, possibly nine today, and the dream of a brand-new cab outside my house, you'd have to bang a symbol around my ears to get my attention lately.

When I walked into the carriage office at Penton Street the whole booking hall was covered in painters' cloths. Hopefully they'll consider a bright summer yellow to lift the mood in this sorry place, but my gut feeling is the military eggshell grey will be deployed once more throughout. As I sat down, checking my suit for speckles of eggshell, Mr O'Connor poked his head round the corner to ask for a Mr Thompson. The three of us in the waiting room looked at each other. No takers. Then, in a cruel twist of fate, we notice his eyebrows draw down and closer together in that, all too common, confused look by those who have just worked out a mistake. 'Oh no, I've just had him' he says, now back on track. 'No, not Thompson, Mr Syme' eyebrows raised looking for an answer. Everyone looks at me. I mean, they're right to, but how did they know.

In I go, head bowed. I take the seat he offers, and all goes quiet. He flicks my file open and says, 'take me from The Archway tavern to the Public Carriage Office'. Its long, and about as wavy as my dad's hair in the sixties. 'Ok, how about Tooting Bec station to the metropolitan tabernacle'. Tooting to the Elephant. I'm all over the place from the last one. 'One more then' he says with no enthusiasm. 'Crowne Place, EC4 to Stamford Road N1'. I'm gone. He's turned up the heat and I'm burning alive in front of him. Obviously, as I walk back to the cloth covered booking hall, I check that it is a D. Of course, it is. I book out and swallowed the disappointment. I'm still close to my Rec, but not closer.

Let's Pretend

Eddie kept his promise. This was a thorough mock test drive. A TX1 was the chosen chariot of the day, and we covered all sorts. Parallel parking, tight corners and in and out with all the disabled ramps with a wheelchair. All seemed to go ok. The wheelchair seat belts were a bit fiddly, but I thought the drive itself was ok. I'd booked my drive for the Barnet test centre and, a few days after seeing Eddie for the mock, was on my way.

When I arrived at Barnet, I had a long wait for them to work out which examiner I would have on the day. This added to an already high nerve count. A nice fella came out to see me in the car park and introduced himself as Dave. The weather was a scorcher and Dave looked like he was due to play Golf straight after seeing me. I done all the pre-drive checks although he had to remind me to 'stick the metre on'. Off we went. As soon as we came out of the test centre a bus had stopped in front of us to pick up a few passengers. Not to waste any time, I indicated around the bus to be greeted with four oncoming vehicles which had to slow and veer over a tad to allow me through. This move itself turned out to be my downfall on the day. Dave had some nice things to say at the end but couldn't see his way through what he saw in the first five minutes of being out on the road with me. I could have done without the failure but, as with this whole path on the Knowledge, you're never safe until you've got that badge. At this rate, I'll be one of those who pass the Knowledge and have the final talk without collecting their badge on the same day. I booked another test straight away. Back up the school, I did a little crying about my misfortune.

My comrades kept my spirits up and I overheard someone saying they were up for their very first 56-day appearance next week. A further appreciation of where I am taking place. I'd taken to not going out on my bike leading right up until my next appearance date. Calling every point sheet that came out and even back to the old days of calling anything I saw on TV or overheard in conversation. Completely immersed in the subject, this was total dedication to the goal. I sat up the school day after day calling those sheets and one day found myself making a cup of tea in the lounge room at Wizann. As I stirred the spoon in my cup the word went out that the draw to see who will host the 2012 Olympics would be screened live for all to see. Every Knowledge boy in the school gathered around that telly waiting eagerly to see if we'd beaten the French to host the greatest show on Earth. As the envelope was opened by the chief official of the Olympic Commission, you could hear a pin drop. I'm sure, up and down the country, all eyes were on that envelope. Suddenly, with what has now become an historic sentence, the official read 'the decision to host the 2012 Olympic games goes to'..........'the city of'.........'London'. The school erupted. Trafalgar Square erupted. The country erupted. At least thirty-five Knowledge boys/girls jumped into the air knowing they have a good chance of playing a real role in the coming games in seven years' time. When I looked around me that day, I felt proud. We're all together doing this madness of the Knowledge. Never knowing what the future will bring in the form of C's or D's (A's and B's were never considered). Clinging to the rumours of the job we're all trying for. United in our love for the subject and the place it's all about. A real warmth filled the room that afternoon.

Syme versus Field

I'm two days away from a possible, mind numbing, nine points. One more appearance after this next one and, unless I lose my frontal lobe memory, I'll be a London Black Cab driver. The phone rings. It's Eddie Sadlier. He informs me that a cancellation has come through for a driving test tomorrow. He reminds me what a great opportunity this could be to pass the test then roll into my coming nine points and put me in a great position of picking up my badge on the same day as all the other new badge holders. 'Ok Eddie, where do you want me?' I say, realising he's made a good point. 'Crawley' he replies, like its round the corner. Crawley? has he checked the distance from Epping to Crawley? I've known people to go closer for their holidays. Anyway, he tells me it's at eleven o'clock, so I'll have a bit of time to get there. Yeah, if I leave in twenty minutes on the sleeper train. I know he's right, so I say yes to it and cancel my other booking later in the month. Hopefully, I'll be putting myself on track and making up for my errors in Barnet with Golfing Dave.

I finally find the test centre right near the Fiveways interchange out there in South London and am greeted by a serious guy. He's got a clip board and a clip-on tie, he means business. All's going well. Disabled ramps and chair. I even stuck the metre on before leaving the test centre.

As we arrived back some half hour later, I mount the kerb causing Mr serious to bang his head off one of the yellow handles. Out of the corner of my eye I can see Eddie flick his cigarette away and plonk his head in his hands almost confirming my fate. I didn't need to be told as I pulled the handbrake up as Mr serious needed the help from a colleague to get him out of the back. Going for the Oscar, I thought his reaction was a little dramatic I must say. I suppose it saved any lengthy explanation of failure.

They finished the painting in the carriage office. A lovely, predictable, eggshell grey. Sitting in the waiting room, I was aghast at a more mature Knowledge boy who seems to be refusing to take off a cowboy hat. He's waiting for an examiner. To have an appearance. Wearing a ten-gallon hat. I'm going to look like teacher's pet compared to the rhinestone cowboy here. Mr Field pokes his head round the door and asks for me. Lovely. Mr Field. A fair man, as we all know. There are a few niceties then we're off. 'Ok, take it easy' he says. 'Take me from the stage door at the Dominion theatre to the Lion King'. Bainbridge street off new Oxford St to Wellington Street in Covent Garden. He's cracking out the stage shows I thought. I'd better look out for the rest of the West End then. Bang, we're outside in a matter of a minute, well, theoretically. He throws another out, just as easy. Then he looks up and say's 'And one last one, the battle of Cable Street to the battle of frith street. Obviously, it's just Cable Street in East London to Frith Street in Soho. One battle involved Oswald Mosley and his fascist black shirts, and the other battle involved the notorious gangsters Jack Spot and Albert Dimes on a street corner in Soho. Although one battle involved hundreds, the latter involved a couple of 60's gangsters tearing shreds out of each other over a gangland feud. Nevertheless, this one didn't take long. The run I mean not the gangland feud, as I believe that took some sorting out. I finished calling the standard three runs and as usual, a little bit of silence heightening the tension. He's got a great big smile on his face as he hands me back my card. Can you believe it, nine points on 21's. In the last couple of months, I've survived a near death experience in Seven Sisters Road. Given concussion to an otherwise healthy driving examiner and risen to the dizzy heights of nine points on 21's. As all the newly famous seem to say nowadays, it's been a roll a coaster of a ride.

Slowly, slowly catchy Monkey

The 'Talk' as they call it, is the presentation of your newly acquired Green Badge by a more senior examiner after all stages of the London Knowledge are complete. The 'Talk' is the very last thing you hear from the public carriage office before you set off into the big wide world of London Cab driving. My next 'Drive' won't be until after my next, and what could be my final, appearance. This is a bit of a blow. The chances of me picking up my badge along with all the other Knowledge boys on the day of our 'Talk' has now become almost impossible when I look at the next available driving test date. I booked the test anyway. Three weeks away. You can usually get into a driving test centre within a reasonable time, but the clouds have gathered again, and I've missed any earlier slots.

See, all things are not sent to triers, they're sent to me.

Very, Very, Very, Very Nice Price

You never know who you're going to get. That's the way it's always been. That's the way it should always stay. Like out there on the streets, you never know who's going to put their hand out and you never know what they're going to say. I was up early. My appearance wasn't until 10am. I was calling over all my sticky lists and most of the blue book from half six that morning. I got the tube down to Angel. Jeff knew the importance of this one and promised to meet me in Penton Street after the judgement. I felt good about what I knew. I didn't stop calling roads, turnings, and points throughout the whole journey down there on the tube. Over the years, I'd done this routine and turning up to appearances so often that I felt almost sad as I walked towards those uninteresting, grey metal doors of the carriage office.

When referring to how he survived twenty-six years in captivity under the apartheid regime, Nelson Mandela said 'no matter how awful something is, the human spirit can get used to it, whether they like it or not'.

To some extent, I'd grown up coming to this place. I booked in with one of the booking clerks. She had worked there as long as I'd been doing the Knowledge, which was about six and a half years by now. She slid my card back to me under the glass partition and momentarily held it there not letting me take it. 'Goodluck' she said with a real smile. They never say anything to you in the booking office. You're just a number they punch. It's so automated that you never see any emotion. For her to even say good luck felt like a guardian angel had spoken. Like some celestial figure had always kept an eye out for me. The mystical shoulder to lean on when times get rough personified in a carriage office booking clerk wearing beige Farah's. This brought a lump to my throat and almost a tear to my eye. I tried not to show any emotion and turned with an attempt at a swagger out of the booking hall only to hit my hand on the door frame. I could've done without that embarrassment, nevertheless I knew comforting forces were at work.

No one is in the waiting room. Just me, on the most important day of my Knowledge life.

Sitting there looking around, I notice the coat stand that I should've put my coat on in my very first appearance with Mrs Sadlier all those years ago. I noticed a square of carpet near the rubbish bin that was once kicked up by a disgruntled knowledge boy on his way out and never replaced. I looked at the big map on the wall that glares at you with an air of superiority, almost beaconing you to take a closer look. The cheap painting of the Gondola, carelessly hung with all its meaning. I had history with this place and, now I could be saying goodbye, the lump in my throat wasn't leaving. Silent, wistfully reflective, I sat and reminisced.

Mr Price, standing there in a grey suit with a very comfortable and, seemingly quiet, pair of hush puppies asked for me to follow him. No formal address, he knew it was me. It all felt strange. I couldn't tell you one part of the journey getting there. Then there was the emotional exchange between me and the booking clerk and now Mr Price has welcomed me with warm familiarity as we walk to his office.

My file was already opened on his desk. He didn't even have to flip it open, as they all usually did. I felt like the whole carriage office had been expecting me. Any minute now, all my previous examiners will come into this room with a cake fully lit with candles to the number of appearances I've had over the years. You're gonna need a bigger cake.

Mr Price, in seen it all fashion, sat down and just said 'this won't take you long, take me from Belgrave Square to Scalini's restaurant. This won't take you long? did I just hear right? I mean he's correct it's only a run that has three roads in really. To say, 'it won't take you long' is like saying 'if you're not doing anything Sunday, you could pop round with the family, my wife's making a rosemary based roast chicken if you fancy it'. I call the run. 'Well done' he says and 'thank you 'I reply. All very polite here. He's not even looking at my file now. He's just got his hands in his lap, saying whatever comes into his mind. 'Trafalgar Square to Vauxhall station?'. He says it like, if you want, you can call this one.

They're all easy runs but what's making it harder for me is the surprisingly relaxed way this is all coming to an end. Then, without even a third run to call he says it. A sentence that I'll never forget. A sentence that, even now, I'll occasionally say to myself to remind me of the impact of those words. 'Congratulations Mr Syme, I'm pleased to tell you, that you have passed the Knowledge of London'.

My head sank into my hands. By the time I'd raised my head, Mr Price had made his way around his desk and was now holding out his hand to shake. I stood up and shook his hand with both of mine. I never wanted to let go. I wanted that handshake to last forever.

He gave me a few forms and advised me to now get the driving test passed and get those suburban runs out of the way in line for my Talk in a few weeks. All this was par for the course. I was filled with love and wanted to tell the world. After booking out I made my way through those double doors out into Penton Street to see Jeff across the road. I ran over to him like a love lost girl on a train platform. With his arms outstretched, I jump right up onto him and, as he caught me, bellowed 'I've done it, I've only done it'. I couldn't get rid of the ear to ear smile I had on my face. I explained everything that had happened that morning. He was well pleased for me, a true friend.

We sat in the star cafe across the road from the carriage office for about an hour as I planned who to call and how to say it.

As Jeff left me to my phone calls out in the street I just couldn't stop laughing whenever I called anyone, family, friends, they were all tearful and my only reaction was an astounded nervous laughter. The release was amazing.

You don't know what's going to happen next, but you are aware that things will now really change in your life. It's the lottery feeling without the big cheque. There's still the little matter of passing that driving test and calling over the suburban runs, but for now, I am the gold medallist, or I should say, the green badge medallist.

Beyond civilisation

After loads of pats on the back, and just as many congratulations from the Knowledge school, I'd set off with my book of suburban runs. Everyone knows by now that you've done the Knowledge, the 'burbs' are just a formality. Nevertheless, there is a chance that the examiner really does want the three or four runs spot on before they finally hand over the badge. Therefore, the pressure still lingers as you really don't want to be held up anymore from 'getting out there' by being asked to come back another day to 'just call those again'.

By now, you've done the knowledge and, it's a known fact, that the green badge has already been made and registered in your name, so you can expect a fair bit a leniency when it comes to your suburban appearance. Anyway. I cracked away at the runs. I found out what lies beyond that one-way system at Catford. I found Pratts Bottom out there in Kent, which is always a pleasure. I reached the delights of north London, whetstone and beyond.

Really, all these extensions of my knowledge were a real pleasure. Driving around, almost going places to be nosey. Knowing that the 'real' Knowledge was safely in the bag was an absolute delight. That achievement feeling kept me alive and kicking during the short spell of 'out the way' runs.

I called those runs a lot during the week of my appearance and even reverted to the old, dinner plate on my lap, role play just to get me in the mood. Leave me alone, I was excited. I knew the date of my driving test was one week after my appearance and, if I got through that, the final 'talk' as well.

A bit of a kick but then again is there any part of expectation that has its upside. I suppose there is if you keep them expectations a lot lower than reality, but this is the Knowledge, low expectation doesn't exist in this town. The day of the appearance, like so many others, was suddenly there. Booked in, no smiles, no flowers just straight into the waiting room.

There are four others sitting down. Then something strange happens. Five examiners fight to get their heads round the door together and all say a different name at once. We all knew who called our name and jumped up and followed our respective examiners, mine being Mr field. He asked me the first three runs of the whole book. Straight off the top. He doesn't want anything else. I call 'em like I've just been reading them, not like I know them, but it doesn't matter. I know fifty thousand other roads and he knows it. He's not bothered that I might be a bit sketchy over Bexley Heath one day or might have to slow down once I get past junction three of the M4 for Heathrow.

Another shake of the hand and Mr field tells me of the procedure for the morning, I'm to go away until midday when I will return to an office that I have never known before in the building and that is where the 'talk' will be. Walking into that room at midday I looked around to find the other four Knowledge boys that were in the waiting room earlier. All there for suburb appearances and, subsequently, their 'talk'.

Mr bishop entered the room. Bishop, known as the chief examiner, took us through what life would be like out there driving around. He ran through a few personal experiences of passengers that he'd taken in his time. He ran through the good and bad personalities that we'll face as life goes on in the cab trade. He covered buying a cab, renting a cab, etiquette amongst drivers, a real overview. There was a bit of humour knocking around amongst us all and any questions at the end of which a few myths and worries were extinguished. Then came the time for everyone, but me, to be handed their green badges by Mr Bishop. He took delight in shuffling the envelopes in front of him and calling out the names of the respected new owners. Even though I knew I wasn't getting my badge there and then it was still a nice feeling to be sitting in that room with the others. They were obviously over the moon at what they were receiving. I felt really pleased for those other four and knew that next week I could have my hands on a green badge with my own number on. Mr Bishop knew that he didn't have one for me and said, once I get the drive done next week, to just pop into the booking hall and go to the licensing window to just collect it over the counter. What? there's other windows in that booking hall?

The day of my latest driving test, my trusty, chain smoking, driving instructor, Eddie, gave me thorough instructions not to hit any kerbs. Not to bump anyone's head and, for god's sake, stick the metre on. The drive went ok. I wasn't overly chuffed but from past tests I knew that was most probably the best I'd done. The examiner wasn't injured in any way, and I wasn't asked to fill out any insurance forms, so I thought I had a chance. Passed. Fantastic.

The next day I went, eagerly for once, to the Carriage Office to collect my badge. It was the first time that I'd ever gone to Penton Street without having an appointment and wondered whether this was an arrestable offence. Anyway, they let me in and up to the second floor I bounced. In fact, since my REC, I'd taken to bouncing almost everywhere.

I queued up at one of the 'other' windows feeling weird. I'm meant to be over there, booking in or out of an appearance, not over here with men that didn't have to wear suits in this place anymore. I posted all the relevant paperwork through the window and then the clerk behind the counter shuffled off and came back with an A5 envelope. I was told to sign something and given a 'good luck' as a goodbye. I turned around and stopped, looked at that A5 envelope and thought, it's in there. Six and a half years and, inside this brown A5 envelope, the prize.

I felt it from the outside first. I didn't want to just rip the envelope open. I wanted to make more of these few moments than the clerk had routinely done. A deep breath and in went my hand and out came a Licensed London Taxi driver all London Green Badge. Brand new. I stood, stared, and voiced the number to myself. 67298. That's me forever now. 67298.

On the other side of the envelope was a post-it note. As I peeled it off, I realised there was something scribbled by the clerk, who gave me the pack. The note read; London awaits! I glanced back and we exchanged smiles.

I couldn't hear anything else in that booking hall for those few seconds. One thing I did hear though, was that immortal sentence from Mr Price a few weeks ago. It's never left me, and never will. 'Congratulations Mr Syme, I'm pleased to tell you, that you have passed the Knowledge of London'.

Printed in Dunstable, United Kingdom